SOMETHING
WICKED

About the Author

Debi Chestnut has been able to see and speak to ghosts her whole life. A paranormal researcher for more than twenty-five years, she gives lectures and conducts workshops to help people better understand paranormal activity. She resides in Michigan.

SOMETHING
WICKED

A Ghost Hunter Explores Negative Spirits

DEBI CHESTNUT

Llewellyn Publications
Woodbury, Minnesota

FIRST EDITION
First Printing, 2016

Cover design: Kevin R. Brown
Cover images: Shutterstock.com/272637416/©perfectlab
Fotolia.com/70578086/©INFINITY

Llewellyn Publications is a registered trademark of Llewellyn Worldwide Ltd.

Psalm 91: New American Standard Bible copyright © 1960, 1962, 1963, 1968, 1971, 1972, 1973, 1975, 1977, 1995 by the Lockman Foundation.

Library of Congress Cataloging-in-Publication Data

Names: Chestnut, Debi, author.

Title: Something wicked : a ghost hunter explores negative spirits / Debi Chestnut.

Description: Woodbury : Llewellyn Worldwide, Ltd, 2016. | Includes bibliographical references and index.

Identifiers: LCCN 2016002267 (print) | LCCN 2016012027 (ebook) | ISBN 9780738742175 | ISBN 9780738748740 ()

Subjects: LCSH: Demonology. | Demoniac possession. | Occultism.

Classification: LCC BF1531 .C44 2016 (print) | LCC BF1531 (ebook) | DDC 133.4/2—dc23

LC record available at http://lccn.loc.gov/2016002267

Llewellyn Publications
A Division of Llewellyn Worldwide Ltd.
2143 Wooddale Drive
Woodbury, MN 55125-2989
www.llewellyn.com

Printed in the United States of America

Other books by Debi Chestnut

Is Your House Haunted?

How to Clear Your Home of Ghosts & Spirits

Stalking Shadows

Contents

INTRODUCTION

I was slightly hesitant when I decided to write this book. I am not an exorcist—I'm a ghost hunter and psychic medium. However, in my travels I have come across a few entities that I would classify as intensely negative, and in a couple of cases, demonic.

There's something different about dealing with demonic entities as compared to the normal ghost, spirit, or negative entity that was once in human form. The situations are more intense—the hauntings and encounters more psychologically, emotionally, and physically violent.

If you're at all sensitive to energy, you can feel it the second you walk into the space that is occupied by a demon. The energy is completely different than if the building or home is occupied by a ghost or spirit—it's more charged, thick, heavy, and you can almost feel something weighing you down, sometimes to the point of feeling oppressed. It sometimes feels like you have to use so much more energy to move, to breathe, to think clearly.

I've never personally seen a person possessed by a demon and I hope I never do, but given the nature of the beast, I have no doubt a demonic entity is fully capable of possession. I have seen demonic hauntings and infestations, which will be covered in a later chapter of this book. I've also seen demons take up residence in homes that are favorable to sustain their existence.

When a demon does take up residence, it doesn't automatically mean that a person in the house is possessed, but it could mean that demonic possession of a living person inside that house is imminent. It could also signal the beginning of a demonic infestation, which can easily lead to possession. Either way it's a serious situation to be sure.

I've written this book in part for those who are interested in the paranormal, but I also kept in mind other ghost hunting teams so they will be prepared if they happen to run into a negative or demonic entity while conducting an investigation.

As for me, I've been able to see and communicate with ghosts and spirits since I was a child, so ghost hunting seemed like a natural fit. I've been ghost hunting for thirty-some years. This has given me the opportunity and honor of seeing and experiencing some things that many other people don't. I've met some very nice ghosts, a few very nasty, negative ghosts, and a handful of very powerful and sometimes negative entities.

I can't say for sure that the very negative entities I met were all demonic. It's my belief that at least one of them was there for another purpose but acted in a manner that could lead someone, at least on the surface, to believe it was demonic.

On a personal note, I didn't believe in demons until I literally had a face-to-face encounter with one. Talk about a gut check. Imagine discovering that your deepest spiritual belief system is seriously flawed and things you didn't believe in, and even go so far as to scoff at, were not only real but standing right in front of you.

This made it impossible for me to deny the existence of demons. Not only did I have to try to wrap my head around having my spiritual belief system seriously challenged, but I had to deal with a creature I was sure didn't exist—all within a matter of seconds.

That was a situation I wouldn't wish on my worst enemy. So my advice would be to forget what you know or think you know about negative entities, such as demons, and take into consideration all points of view, all the evidence of their existence—the folklore, urban legends, and mythology; for even in the most bizarre story, there is a grain of truth if you look for it hard enough. Explore the topic of negative energies, dark forces, and exorcisms with fresh eyes and an open mind, then come to your own conclusions. In other words, do your research, think about what you've learned—educate yourself. In the world of negative beings and demonic entities, knowledge and your faith are your biggest weapons and your source of strength.

My main goal in writing this book was to give information, and perhaps a warning, on what demonic creatures do, how they behave, how they infest and possess, and what to look for before the situation gets out of control. There is pure evil that lurks in the universe just waiting for an invitation or opportunity to strike.

The sources for the stories of exorcisms and the names of everyone involved have been changed—those people have been victimized enough and there's no good reason to victimize them again.

For the purposes of this book, I'm going to mainly stay with the Catholic/Christian view of demons because that is the social norm and what most people are most familiar with.

Now, let's get to the good stuff.

Happy Hauntings,
Debi Chestnut

DEMONS

The very word "demon" evokes a gut reaction in most people. Either people believe in them or they don't. If they don't, then nothing short of meeting one face-to-face is going to change their mind and that's okay.

The truth is it doesn't matter whether or not you believe in Satan or demons. In fact, demons themselves prefer you don't believe in their existence, because demons can cloak themselves, which enables them to tempt or deceive people without having any blame. After all, you don't believe in demons, right? See how it works?

It's been my experience that unless you are one of the few who have encountered a demon, it's almost impossible to grasp the depth and scope of such pure evil and how these creatures can enter someone's life and completely turn that person's life upside down. If that person is lucky enough to survive such an encounter they come out the other side different—forever changed. They are emotionally, psychologically, and in some cases, spiritually broken. It can take months, but more likely years, for someone to recover from such an experience. To be perfectly honest, I believe that people don't ever really recover from having their life invaded by a demonic entity.

If you're like me—part of a ghost hunting team—or if you're just a person going about your business and a demon enters your life—it's important to know exactly what you believe. Speaking from experience I can tell you, in some cases, it's going to be your faith in whatever supreme being(s) you believe in that's going to get you through.

While many people around the world believe in the existence of demons and their ability to possess, the approaches to deal with them are different. The ways demons are handled around the world shows us that no matter what the method, there isn't a right or wrong way to deal with a demon, as long as the method is effective and the ritual performed, whatever that may be, is done by someone qualified in that belief system to do so.

It also shows us that in many ways all religions are equal on some level and none are better or worse than the other. As long as a person's chosen religion works for them and for that segment of society, religion can become a deep and meaningful part of a person's and society's belief system.

The ghost hunting team I belong to has members from many different religions. We have members who are Buddhists, atheists, Catholics, Wiccans, Christians, and Pagans. Each member brings something important to the table and to our team because of who they are and their religious belief systems, or lack thereof, in some cases. Regardless of religious affiliation, it is the coming together as a group for a common goal and to share our knowledge and beliefs that makes the team work. This is what makes our job as paranormal investigators safer and more productive, especially if we run into a negative entity or a demon.

The evil one, as Satan is often referred to in some religious circles, had a very prominent place in people's imaginations during the time of Jesus Christ. As was the custom of the day, Satan was blamed for a plethora of mental illnesses and other maladies.

In addition, Jesus used Satan as the poster child for evil powers to give Jesus material for his parables. Some scholars believe that to Jesus, Satan was just a symbol of all things evil or morally wrong.

In the first epistle of St. Peter, it's said that the world remains in the power of Satan until the prophecy contained in the second advent of Christ is fulfilled and that we had better be prepared for Satan's onslaught. Demons are insidious, vile creatures that, according to many Christian sects, are fallen angels led by Lucifer. Christians and scholars who study the Holy Bible have come up with many theories as to why Lucifer rebelled against God.

Some people believe that Lucifer was too prideful and arrogant—that he didn't want to follow God's rules. Others believe that Lucifer became jealous of humans and felt that God loved humans more than the angels. There are other people who believe that Lucifer became outraged over the fact that while God gave humans free will, the angels were not given the same.

Still another theory is that even though Satan was the highest-ranking angel under God, he didn't want to be under God, but wanted to be God and to rule the entire universe and, in turn, this is what caused Satan to be cast out of heaven. The list of possibilities is endless.

Whatever the reason and whatever you personally believe, the result is the same. Lucifer and some other angels rebelled and after a brief but fierce angel war, were cast out of heaven and into what we call hell. One story says that it was the mighty

Archangel Michael who, under the order of God, was the one to raise his sword and cast Lucifer and his dominions out of heaven.

Personally, I go with the Archangel Michael scenario, because the Prayers to Archangel Michael are specifically designed to cast out demons. I've used these prayers to protect myself and my ghost hunting team—I know they work.

Lucifer, or Satan, as he is sometimes called, has been blamed for many things throughout history. These things include but aren't limited to: sickness, deformities, welts, boils, blindness, convulsions, and epilepsy, and natural disasters such as tornados, hurricanes, and earthquakes, just to name a few.

Is a demon capable of these things? Let's just say it's possible. Has a demon caused all these horrible things all the time? Not a chance.

People have been practicing the rites of exorcism since ancient times and they are still part of many religions and cultures today. The term "exorcism" comes from the Latin word *exorcismus*, which means "to adjure." Basically it is the practice of driving demons or other evil entities from a place or person that is deemed to be possessed.

Many of the exorcists who perform these rituals believe they have a calling from God or whatever supreme power they believe in. In some cultures, it's believed that exorcists have some sort of special power or gift that allows them to drive out the evil that has taken up residence inside a person, building, or plot of land.

The whole premise of possession was born from prehistoric shamanistic beliefs. Many religious texts, such as the Hebrew

Bible, the New Testament, and the Vedas (the holy books of the Hindus), all contain exorcisms.

The number of exorcisms being performed around the world has declined over the years because of the advancement of psychology and the knowledge that many of the people who once would have been exorcised really have a mental illness or other malady.

However, within the last few years there has been a resurgence of exorcisms and many people, myself included, find this fact particularly disturbing on many levels. One real danger is that just about anybody can call themselves an exorcist or demonologist and in many cases could be doing more harm than good—no matter what their intentions.

These so-called "exorcists" are, in some cases, charging people a lot of money to perform an exorcism when they aren't trained or qualified to even perform the Rites of Exorcism, let alone take the proper steps to ensure the person who claims to be possessed isn't suffering from a mental illness or other type of sickness.

Because paranormal research is not an accepted science, there are no regulations, or moral and/or ethical rules, that govern this field of "fringe" science, as it's sometimes called. While many people offer classes with certifications online and in some other types of educational facilities, none of them are really legitimate, because there isn't any type of certification available in the paranormal field—although in many cases the classes do offer good and valuable information. I personally know of only one online class taught by a qualified person—he is a Catholic Bishop.

Also, with the recent trend in movies, some books, and television shows that tend to depict and/or glorify dark creatures such as vampires, werewolves, and demonic forces, the increase in demonic activity really should surprise no one. But many people in the paranormal and religious communities are becoming increasingly alarmed—and they should be.

Personally I've been shocked by the sheer number of emails I receive from people who are dabbling in the occult and paranormal. Generally the emails are asking for answers to questions or they are curious about paranormal experiences they've had. However, some of the emails are from people who have experimented with the paranormal and have gotten themselves into a paranormal situation they can't handle and are looking for help in getting out of it.

In my opinion, people should be more up-front about their paranormal experiences and problems and be more willing to talk openly about this topic. With mainstream media, television, and movies putting forth information and theories that are inaccurate, society as a whole needs to take on this topic and be more vocal about the paranormal and bring forth information that is based in truth, validity, and substance.

In addition, if there is a rise in demonic infestations and possessions, and it wouldn't surprise me if there were, then it could mean any number of things. For example, people may be involved in something they shouldn't be, or dabbling in something they know very little about. In addition, some people may not believe demons are real and may be inadvertently inviting them into their space, causing an upswing in demonic activity.

It could also mean that the Seven Seals of the Apocalypse, as outlined in the Book of Revelations, are being opened one by one as negative changes in global society catapult the human race towards Armageddon.

Take your pick—they're all good reasons, and valid arguments can be made for each one of them.

Although many people believe such creatures are things of
folklore, literature, and religious mythology—and granted, some
of them are fictitious creations—I can assure you that demons
and other dark forces are very real and are not creatures to be
trifled with. The truth of the matter is: Just because you don't
believe in something, doesn't mean it doesn't exist.

TYPES OF
NEGATIVE ENTITIES

When some people hear the term "negative entity" they automatically assume the reference is to a demon. In some cases this would be correct, and while demons are one of the only entities that can truly possess someone, there are a few different types of demons, as well as negative entities. The one thing demons and other types of negative spirits have in common is that they can hurt you and, in some cases, even kill you unless the situation is handled before it gets to that point.

The one thing that sets demons apart from other types of negative entities is that they are considered to be inhuman, meaning they were never alive in a human body. This holds true for some other types of negative entities such as elementals. However, there are some types of negative entities that once were human, such as an avenger.

As this chapter shows, there are many different types of negative entities, both human and inhuman, that are more than capable of causing harm to the living, but in my opinion, none are as lethal and dangerous as a demon.

Negative entities that were once in human form can at least be reasoned with to some degree, and if handled properly, can be expelled from your life once the type of ghost or spirit is identified properly and their reason for being there becomes clear.

However, inhuman entities are another story. No matter what type of inhuman phantom a person may encounter, generally the reasons for the inhuman phantom being there are notoriously evil, and getting rid of them can be exceedingly difficult.

Whether a once-human or inhuman negative entity, getting rid of a negative entity of any type should only be handled by someone trained to deal with such negative specters.

It's important not to jump to conclusions when it comes to any type of ghost or spirit, be it a negative one or not. It's been my experience that many people automatically associate many types of paranormal activity with a demon. Keep in mind that demonic hauntings are extremely rare. By assuming a demonic entity is present, one could unintentionally lure a negative entity, such as a demon, to a home where there really wasn't anything but a normal ghost.

What people need to understand is that unless your life has been personally invaded by a demon or some of the other types of negative entity, it's almost impossible to understand fully how profoundly it changes a person emotionally, psychologically, and spiritually.

As I sit here writing, the light coming in from my window is fading to the color of smoke and the various creatures afraid of the daylight are coming out to hunt, so let's begin.

Poltergeists

In German, the word "poltergeist" literally means "noisy ghost," and they certainly are that.

There are some paranormal investigators who believe that poltergeists are a form of demon. Although I wouldn't necessarily agree with that line of thought, I could be persuaded that poltergeists could be a form of inhuman that doesn't fall into the demonic entity category.

There is really no rhyme or reason to where they show up, how they show up, and why they show up. In many cases, they depart as quickly as they came, leaving a path of destruction in their wake, although no one is exactly sure why they choose to leave when they do.

Poltergeists are capable of throwing things and making things disappear only to reappear, sometimes in a different place all together. They can open and close doors and cupboards, they can move heavy objects with ease, and they can stack dining room chairs in many interesting variations. Poltergeists can bang on walls, make the sound of footsteps, and turn on and off faucets, televisions, radios, computers, and just about any other appliance, device, or object you can think of.

As an example, I was contacted by a couple who were dealing with an exceptionally vindictive and violent poltergeist. They reported to me activity such as dishes and other objects flying off of shelves, countertops, and tables; being pushed and shoved on different occasions; and hearing rapping, scratching, and pounding on doors, walls, and windows at all hours of the night.

I spoke with this couple at length and told them I would come investigate the situation. I also warned them that sometimes if an entity knows someone is coming to help, the activity might increase because the entity is either scared, angry, or excited.

On a cold, windy afternoon I pulled up in front of a cookie-cutter house in a nice, quiet suburb of Detroit. When I got out of my car and began walking up the sidewalk I could feel the energy radiating from inside the house out towards me. The energy felt heavy, angry, and I knew immediately my presence there wasn't one the poltergeist was welcoming by any stretch of the imagination.

It became hard for me to push through the energy to the front door, it literally felt like I was trying to walk through mud, but I persevered and climbed the two cement steps to the small porch and rang the doorbell.

The young couple answered and stepped back so I could enter their home. Just as I crossed the threshold, a long-bladed knife came flying out of the kitchen towards me and lodged itself in the doorjamb just to the left side of my head.

Naturally the young couple screamed in horror, and I have to admit my first instinct was to run, but knowing that any sign of fear or weakness on my part would let the poltergeist win, I held my ground. As calmly as possible I reached up and pulled the knife out of the doorjamb and I addressed the entity directly: "Is that the best you got?"

Almost immediately the energy in the house shifted dramatically. It began to feel less chaotic, less heavy, and went from a loud, crushing energy to barely a whisper. In other words, by my taking control of the situation and not showing fear, the poltergeist backed off and calmed down. Once I accomplished that, I did a slow walk-through of the home in order to confirm that I was dealing with a poltergeist and not another entity such as a ghost, spirit, or demon.

Poltergeists generally will not communicate with a psychic medium like a ghost, spirit, or demon will, and this one was no exception. I opened all lines of communication and adjusted my energy to match the same frequency as the poltergeist, but to no avail.

Having no other choice, I performed the prayers and rituals I normally would use in this type of situation to rid the home of the pesky poltergeist. Once I was satisfied it was gone, I left. A few weeks later the couple called and told me that everything was fine and there wasn't any sign that the poltergeist had returned.

This just goes to show that poltergeists can be dangerous and, intentionally or sometimes unintentionally, attempt to physically harm a living person.

As I said before, it's been my experience that a poltergeist normally doesn't make any attempt to communicate with the living like other types of entities, and most attempts at communication with a poltergeist will normally go unanswered. However, in some cases, attempting to communicate with a poltergeist could result in a drastic and generally short-lived increase in paranormal activity.

The damage a poltergeist can do is not just physical. Poltergeist activity can be terrifying and the effect this type of activity can have over time on a living person can be emotionally draining and psychologically damaging.

Sometimes the activity will center around one person. This has led some scientists to believe that if a teenager resides in the home experiencing the poltergeist activity, that many poltergeists are an outward manifestation of the teenager's hormones, stress, frustration, and energy, all without the teenager aware they are doing this.

While I'm sure this is possible in some instances, I have a hard time believing that all poltergeist activity can be explained away this easily, especially in the cases where there's not a teenager or any other children living in the home.

It's a generally accepted theory in the paranormal community that poltergeists never had any physical or emotional ties to the place they choose to take up residence. Therefore they are one of the hardest types of entities to get rid of. Normally one just has to let the activity run its course and slowly die out over time, if the activity stops at all. Not the best solution, to be sure, but sometimes it's the only option and there appears to be no rhyme or reason to a poltergeist's appearance or departure.

As you can clearly see there is a lot of controversy and many unanswered questions regarding poltergeists. One has to assume that if they're classified as demons by some people and a form of ghost or spirit by others then poltergeists would also have to be considered an intelligent entity—meaning they interact in some way with the living. Even if the method they use is generally manipulating some physical object or imitating sounds such as footsteps, music, screaming, scratching, etc., it is still a form of communication and could also be considered a form of interaction with the living.

As for how poltergeists take up residence in a place where they don't appear to have an emotional or physical attachment, I can offer up a couple of possible scenarios.

While a poltergeist may not be attached to the location, there's nothing that says this type of entity couldn't be attached to something else that is brought into the location, i.e., a haunted object.

Haunted objects, or objects with a type of entity attached to them, are not uncommon. I am in possession of a few such objects and there are many people who collect these objects, although for the life of me I can't figure out exactly why. The haunted objects I have in my possession are things that were given to me by some of my clients, and I do what I can to release or coax the ghost or spirit out of the object and get them to cross over.

Also, it's very possible that people are unknowingly purchasing haunted items from flea markets, antique stores, estate sales, thrift stores, etc. and bringing them into their homes. Once there, the entity or poltergeist that's using the object as a vessel is free to cause chaos in that person's home and would have no physical or emotional tie to that location because their attachment is to the object itself, not that specific location. The activity would suddenly stop if the ghost or spirit in the object decided to cross over or the living person got rid of the object the entity was attached to.

Another distinct possibility is a form of mild spirit attachment. In this scenario the poltergeist would be a form of parasitic entity that attaches to a person and literally is brought into that person's home without the person being aware it's even there—until it starts causing some form of paranormal activity. Even then it would be hard for that person to figure out how that entity got there.

It would be easy for the ghost or spirit to detach from the living person and either leave on its own at a time of its choosing, or for it to be forced out by a skilled paranormal investigator or someone skilled in dealing with poltergeists.

Avengers

While an avenger is a spirit that was once alive in human form, they can be a dangerous threat to their intended target. An avenger is strictly out for revenge and their target is someone who they feel wronged them some way when they were alive. It would be very rare for someone other than their target to be harmed, but not impossible, because sometimes an innocent person can get caught in the crossfire.

This type of spirit cannot possess a person. However, they can become extremely violent and in rare cases cause their target to die. As an example, this may be achieved by pushing the target in front of a car or train, or down a flight of stairs. Thus the reason they are included in this book.

If the avenging spirit has returned to get revenge for their death, such as a murder victim, etc., they may appear at the scene of the crime or to a trusted loved one in an attempt to tell them that their death was not an accident or in an attempt to communicate who killed them. The avenging spirit will not stop until they feel justice has been served or their appetite for revenge sated in some way.

An avenging spirit will also generally appear in the same clothes they wore when they were alive and can be male or female. It wouldn't be uncommon for an avenging spirit to appear as a full-body apparition.

Because of the type of behavior an avenging spirit is capable of displaying, many times they are mistaken for a poltergeist. One distinguishing factor may be that the activity will be targeted towards one person in the household while the other members of the family will be left alone.

While an avenging ghost is pretty rare, occasionally a story of one will come my way, and when it does, it captures my attention. Just recently I heard about an avenging spirit out in what was once the old West. Apparently this man, when alive, was hung for robbing a stagecoach and other such crimes. The story goes that he was hunted down by the sheriff and a few other men and then brought to justice.

Since that time, some of the descendants of the people who captured this outlaw have died under some rather seemingly innocent circumstances. For example, one was hit by a car; one young man suffered a heart attack while jogging; a young woman was murdered; and another perfectly healthy woman died from complications due to childbirth. All of these deaths appear to have some form of logical explanation; what sets them apart from other deaths like these is all of these victims reported experiencing some form of paranormal activity in the weeks or months leading up to their deaths.

There's speculation that the deaths were caused by the man their long-lost relative brought to justice many years ago. So the question remains: normal deaths or the work of an avenging spirit? It just seems to be a little odd that all of these deaths were from the same families—generation after generation.

Not all avenging spirits act out to this degree and one could speculate that the harshness of the revenge could be dependent on what type of wrong the spirit feels was committed against them when they were alive.

In some cases it may be possible to simply apologize for one's actions and the spirit may be satisfied with that and leave.

However, in most of the avenging spirit cases I've heard about, this type of spirit can be difficult to get rid of before their thirst for revenge is sated and almost any attempt to reason with this type of entity can prove to be fruitless, although depending on the spirit, it can be done.

Parasitic Entities

A parasitic entity is a type of spirit that attaches itself to a person and may be also referred to as a spirit attachment in some paranormal circles. There are some parasitic spirits that are not out to harm, while others are out to destroy.

For example, a human spirit that attaches to a person, while still dangerous, is not as bad as a non-human form of parasitic entity, which many paranormal investigators categorize as a form of demon.

Living people suffering from a spirit attachment may experience extreme nightmares, lack of motivation, dizziness, unclear thought patterns, and could form an addiction to drugs, alcohol, or another type of negative activity that is totally out of character for them.

The goal of some parasitic entities, mostly non-humans, is to suck the energy out of a human body. When this happens, the living person's immune system can become extremely weak and make them more likely to get sick. Depending on how weak the living person is and how long the parasitic entity has been attached to them, any illness could result in death.

If you're experiencing any of the above symptoms of a parasitic entity attachment, don't freak out; it doesn't necessarily mean that any type of spirit has attached to you. In fact, parasitic entity attachments are not very common. The trademark signs of a parasitic attachment are also common symptoms of many medical illnesses. If you are suffering some of the symptoms of a parasitic entity attachment, you should go to your doctor to make sure you are not suffering from a physical, mental, or emotional issue.

It's important to note that just because a spirit is around, it doesn't mean they are attached to you in the form of a parasitic entity. For example, the spirit of a loved one who is deceased may be close to you and make themselves known in certain ways that are not a threat to your health or well-being, whereas a parasitic entity is literally attached to your body like a leech.

How a parasitic entity chooses who they attach to is the subject of debate among paranormal researchers. Some people believe there is really no rhyme or reason for a parasitic entity to be attracted to one person over another. Others in the paranormal community believe that in the case of a human parasite, the person they choose to attach to may have a habit the entity had in life and misses in death. For example, smoking, drinking, drug addiction—the list is practically endless, but the examples listed are among the most common thought to attract a parasitic entity.

When it comes to non-human parasitic entities, it can get even more confusing as to why they would choose one particular person. The most common belief is that because they can be classified as a type of demon and they sense a weakness or vulnerability in a particular person that makes it easy to attach to their chosen target.

Recently I consulted on a case of a parasitic entity attachment. The case involved a teenager who was in terrible shape because of some type of entity attached to her. When the symptoms first started, she would experience headaches and drastic mood swings. In addition, she would suffer from frightening nightmares that involved a "dark man," as she called him, every night would come up with very gruesome and painful ways to murder her. These nightmares continued and intensified during the time the entity was attached to her. The attachment became so severe that by the time the parents contacted me, their daughter could no longer walk.

Her parents had taken her to various doctors and hospitals in attempt to find a physical ailment that was causing this mysterious illness, but all the tests came back as normal.

Once I was contacted and knew the severity of the problem, I called on another team that I'd worked with. This team specializes in such entities and we worked together to solve the problem.

This team had the parents do various rituals, blessings, and house clearings until everything was in place to remove the entity. Various mediums and other psychic and paranormal specialists worked from pictures of the girl to determine that the entity attached to her was a large spider-like creature who had its tentacles deeply attached to the young woman.

Through various techniques this team was able to remove the attachment and within a week the teenager was feeling great, was able to walk normally, and all nightmares had stopped.

Keep in mind this was an extreme case and very rare. While I'm not sure what type of entity was attached to this young woman, I am sure that this entity probably never existed in human form.

Elementals

Elementals are thought to be some type of nature spirits. While generally these types of entities are thought to be simply myth and legend in folklore, fairies, leprechauns, elves, and other types of beings are believed to be grouped in the elemental category. To some people elementals are extremely real and in some instances can be dangerous.

Elementals are so steeped in many cultures that long before any formal religions were formed, people believed in the existence of elementals. However, most of the Christian religions convinced people that because they couldn't be seen, elementals didn't exist.

In some religions, elementals rule over the elements of earth, air, fire, and water, with each separate elemental having their own unique and distinguishable characteristics.

In many circles it is believed that elementals can be summoned by voodoo, hoodoo, and other forms of chaos magic, just to name a few. It's also believed that an elemental, like a demon, will not take up residence without being invited to do so.

Once summoned and given a purpose, the elemental will continue to perform its duties until told or made to stop. Some people in the paranormal world believe that all elementals are negative entities, an opinion I don't necessarily agree with.

I believe that if an elemental is summoned and given a particular task, such as to protect a location and/or person, the elemental will resort to any means necessary to complete its assigned mission. Therefore, the mere act of completing its mission could involve violent activity, which could be perceived as being demonic in nature.

Right or wrong, good or bad, light or dark, I don't believe an elemental makes that distinction. I think an elemental will resort to some drastic measures in order to carry out their assigned mission. This doesn't necessarily make them a demon, but it can make them a negative entity that can cause serious physical harm to the living if pushed far enough.

I had an occasion to come in contact with what I believed to be an elemental a few years ago. The case involved a pre–Civil War barn.

The barn itself had a dirt floor and two lofts—one on each side of the barn. It also contained a tack room, workroom, and several stalls for horses. The owner of the property reported that so many of his horses refused to enter the barn and reacted violently when he tried to put them in the barn that he finally gave up and built a new barn behind the historic barn in question. The horses, of course, had no trouble entering or exiting the new barn, but gave the old barn a wide berth every time they went near it.

When the owner of the barn decided to install running water in the barn that was now mostly being used as a workroom and storage, he began to dig a trench in the dirt floor from the back of the barn to the workroom at the front of the barn. In order to do that he had to dig the trench through a horse stall, down a hallway, and then make a sharp right to get to the workroom.

When he got to the end of the hallway, his shovel hit something buried in the dirt. He carefully removed the loose dirt and uncovered two small bundles wrapped in faded, handmade blankets. He gently unwrapped the bundles and discovered the skeletons of two small babies.

Just as he got the second baby unwrapped, some unseen force grabbed him from behind and threw him effortlessly about thirty feet across the barn. As you can imagine, this experience was terrifying, but he had the peace of mind to rewrap and re-bury the two babies before making a fast exit from the barn.

Over the course of the next several months he had various paranormal investigators out to investigate the barn, but each time either one of the investigators would be levitated and thrown out of the barn, or some long iron pipes stored in the rafters would be thrown at them. It was at this point he contacted the leader of the team I belong to.

We conducted extensive research on the barn, the city where the barn was located, and on the property itself. The owner of the property, however, gave us the final piece of the puzzle. He said that he was able to learn from the former property owners that the barn was once a stop on the Underground Railroad and housed escaped slaves until they could safely make their way into Canada. Being that the property was so close to the Michigan-Canadian border, this information made historical sense to us.

Using that information, our hypothesis was one or two of the slave women gave birth to babies that either were stillborn or died shortly after birth. The women then gently wrapped them in blankets and buried them in the dirt floor of the barn.

Given that many slaves practiced voodoo or hoodoo, it would only be natural for them to summon an elemental to protect their babies. Therefore, the elemental would have just been doing its job when it threw the owner and others across the barn.

We found out from the owner that all the paranormal teams that entered the barn were intent on getting rid of the entity.

So, what was really happening was that the elemental was defending not only the babies as it was summoned to do, but also defending itself from extermination.

This information was invaluable to us, because it gave us a leg up in getting close to the elemental without causing it to attack and potentially harm any team members. When we cautiously entered the barn I told the entity that we weren't there to get rid of it, we simply wanted to know its story so that we could better understand its position. We made our way through the workroom and stalls without incident. We then turned our attention to the loft area. We'd set up night-vision video recorders on one side of the loft that would shoot the loft on the opposite side of the barn.

We also discovered that the owner's son often played in the loft of the barn, because there were a bunch of tennis balls and an automatic pitching machine in the loft.

Upon discovering this, we talked to the owner, who said his son never experienced anything paranormal in the barn. This made sense to us, because if our theory was correct and the elemental was summoned to protect the babies, then it would be only natural that the elemental would also view the owner's son as a child and would protect him as well—not harm him.

During the night we investigated there were several times I had an interesting interaction with the elemental, each time up in the loft. The loft itself was pitch black; I could barely see my hand in front of my face, and other team members appeared only as vague blacker-than-ink shadows—and then only if they were standing right next to me.

As I was standing in the loft peering across the expanse of the barn to the other loft, looking for any signs of movement, I saw a dark figure standing right next to me. Assuming it was my investigation partner, I reached out my hand to touch his arm, but when I did, my hand went right through the dark figure! It was the elemental, standing next to me, and I didn't even know it! This happened several times throughout the evening and I got the sense that the elemental was enjoying this little game of cat-and-mouse as much as we were.

We left the barn late that night and made no attempt whatsoever to get rid of the mysterious entity that roamed its empty stalls and hallways, protecting the bodies and spirits of the dead babies, but also protecting the living and breathing son of the owner.

This is why it's so very important to try to understand what you're dealing with before going into a location, and find out as much information as possible—not only about the property, but about other paranormal investigations that may have taken place and how those teams handled the situation.

Incubus and Succubus

An incubus is a form of male demon that comes to the earthly plane to have sex with women who are alive. Its counterpart, the succubus, is the female version who has sex with living men. There is a belief among some cultures and religions that a person can be visited more than once by such a creature. It is also widely accepted in the paranormal world that they are inhuman spirits, meaning they've never been alive on earth.

In some religions it is believed that repeated visitations by an incubus or succubus can cause death because the living person it is attracted to could become so weak that they will get sick and die.

Throughout some parts of Europe it was widely accepted that if a child was conceived between the living and an incubus that child could be born with a mental illness or physical deformity, or grow up to be a witch or warlock.

In medieval times the belief in incubi and succubi was so widespread that a woman who got pregnant because of an extramarital affair she would blame an incubus in order to hide the affair. In addition, rapists would blame an incubus in order to avoid punishment or prison time.

During the Middle Ages, many rapes of women by priests or others in positions of trust were blamed on a paranormal event such as an incubus. Although there are still reports of people being attacked by an incubus or succubus, there is a heated debate between the medical field and paranormal investigators about the existence of incubi and succubi, because when a person is being attacked by this type of entity they can't move or scream until the attack is over.

The debate is whether or not the person was truly attacked by this form of demon or whether they were suffering from sleep paralysis.

Sleep paralysis occurs during the REM period of sleep. The body will release specific hormones that paralyze it to prevent the person from acting out their dreams and possibly harming themselves. There are times when we wake up before the hormones have completely worn off, which then leaves the person unable to move and feeling as if there is an evil presence in the room.

The symptoms of sleep paralysis are almost identical to that of an attack by an incubus and/or succubus—hence the debate.

The person who had this experience will swear they were being attacked by a demon while the doctors will simply write off the experience as sleep paralysis—sometimes a little too quickly. Most people in the paranormal community will accept the premise of sleep paralysis; however, they aren't as quick to write off the possibility of an attack by an incubus, succubus, or another type of demon, and they take the matter very seriously.

Personally I keep an open mind when it comes to the existence of an incubus and/or succubus. There may be many types of entities that we may not know about or know very little about. So the possibility of an incubus or succubus cannot be dismissed without further knowledge and investigation.

Demons

When you've been ghost hunting as long as I have, you've pretty much seen it all—the ghosts and spirits of those who were once alive, moving objects, dark shadows—the list goes on and on. Each ghost hunt and every ghost is new and unique.

However, occasionally I'll run across something that has never been alive. These are the inhumans or nonhumans. As previously discussed, this class of phantom can range from a parasitic entity to an elemental, and, of course, demons and/or demon-like entities.

While inhuman entities are extremely rare, they are out there and anyone whose life has ever been touched by one of these entities will tell you—they are very real. These same people will probably also tell you that the demonic entity turned their lives upside down and made their very existence a living hell.

In many Christian religions, a demon's only goal is to turn the living person away from God. While I won't even try to dispel this belief, personally I believe their goal is more insidious and extreme. I feel that a demon's goal is to destroy the living human they've chosen as their victim; to strip away their free will, their will to live, and to make the living person totally surrender to being controlled by the demon.

Is the demon out to steal their victim's soul? I don't know—I'm not even sure that can be done. All I do know is that demons are capable of unbelievable things and wield extreme power; if left unchecked, a demon is also very capable of killing their victim.

If indeed Lucifer and some of the other angels were angry at God because He gave humans the freedom of choice and the angels were not bestowed with this gift, then to take away a human's free will would be the ultimate in satisfaction for the fallen angel and/or demon, and a direct affront to God.

There are many paranormal investigators and members of clergy who believe that by speaking a demon's name you are summoning it to you, or calling it into your home in some way.

Personally I believe the opposite is true. It's my opinion that if you know the name of the demonic entity you are dealing with, it gives you some measure of power over the demon. Don't get me wrong, knowing the name of the demon that has invaded your life doesn't even the playing field—not even a little bit. But psychologically it can be a big boost and make you feel like you have some control over your life, which is probably spinning wildly out of control because of the demon.

I also believe that knowing the name of the demonic entity puts it on notice and lets the demon know that you know what it is and who it is. This is important because demons are capable of appearing as anyone they choose. For example, a demon could appear as a deceased parent, grandparent, friend, etc. It does this because, in order for the demon to move into your home, it has to be invited in some way. In other words, you have to trust it enough to accept its presence in your life. What better way to do that than appearing as someone you loved who has passed away?

More about how demons behave and operate once they come into a person's life will be discussed in other chapters.

Several years ago, I worked on a case involving a possible demon. I say "possible" because there were several other spirits occupying the property. One of the entities, when he was alive, had been extremely abusive and it was possible but unlikely that he was the cause of the activity in the home—the target of which seemed to be a single mother and one of her teenage children.

If, in fact, this entity was a demon, and I believe it was, then what's important to note is that the property and accompanying acreage carried with it a mysterious and dark history, which was what could have lured the entity to this location in the first place.

While we couldn't verify the data, this was what we believed to be the history of the property based upon local tales, newspaper accounts, and personal accounts from some of the townsfolk: Back in the late 1960s to the mid-1970s, there was an old church located on a piece of property. When the church was deserted by its parishioners it was eventually taken over by a group of people who worshipped Satan. While no one knew or was saying what actually went on in this church, we would be drawn to believe that the possibility existed that dark masses, animal sacrifice, and other Satanic activities took place there.

Eventually the church was deserted by the Satan worshipers and it's believed either their location was discovered or the group disbanded. One story we heard said that the church burned to the ground and the group simply moved to a new location.

The homeowner told us that the remains of an old church were on the acreage, but given the time of day—it was close to nightfall—we didn't have time to explore the tens of acres where the church possibly stood, and the homeowner couldn't remember—or wouldn't disclose the exact location.

EVPs (electronic voice phenomena) and the experiences of the family led us to believe the entity was centered in the basement around an old fieldstone wall that separated two rooms from each other. It appeared, given the location of this fieldstone wall, that the house was added onto at some point and additional basement space added below the addition.

The homeowner said she'd heard a rumor that a body was buried inside that stone wall, but we found no evidence to prove or disprove that tale and dismissed it as a local legend.

It's also important to know that the daughter who was being bothered by the entity was on anti-depressants, and like many teenagers was rather rebellious.

We conducted a prolonged investigation and came in contact with several spirits, including the spirits of two small children. One of the child spirits told me that she and her brother, mother, and father were being held there against their will by the "mean man in the basement" of the house. They were scared and wanted to leave.

The little girl spirit also told me that there were two other spirits besides them and the man in the basement at the property: One was an older man who was trying to protect the family and the other was a man who hung out in the shed where his workroom used to be when he was alive and lived in the home.

While I still wasn't entirely convinced the entity in the basement was a demon, it was a negative energy and needed to be eliminated from the property.

I set up what I needed to conduct an extraction of the spirit, and when I walked by the ghost box—a ghost communication device—that my team member had left running, a man's menacing voice came out of the ghost box and said, "You're going to die!"

I stopped and calmly replied, "Yes, I am, but not tonight."

It took less than an hour to complete the extraction and send the other spirits, who were being held there by the negative entity, into the light.

The family has not reported any additional activity to me or any other member of the team. However, I can't help but wonder if the remains of the old church on the property hold more evil that eventually will work its way into the home.

Demons as Mythology

There are skeptics who don't believe God, angels, demons, and other types of entities even exist—they view religion as a type of mythology. Their argument does have some merit. For example, organized religions are man-made, created by people who may have had ulterior motives.

Some people believe that in the Christian religion, demons were introduced to keep people in line—to control them in some way by making them believe that something bad or evil was going to happen to them if they didn't follow the rules of the religion.

It's important to remember that in ancient times when some religions were just taking shape, society was much different than it is today. People didn't have an understanding of the world as a whole, including society, sickness, the weather, and other natural disasters. In other words, they needed something to explain the world around them that made sense—hence, religion.

The early religious leaders would use good and evil not only to teach lessons but to keep the citizens in line, which helped maintain a certain amount of order in society and in the separate religions.

I'm not saying I believe that God and His creations are all made up and have become woven into the pattern of our world to the point that they have become real. I think it's a matter of faith, belief, life experiences, etc. It's a matter of having the ability to explore the world around us and form our own opinions.

While every culture and civilization has had and will continue to have its own folklore, legends, stories, and some type of religion, to each culture their religion is very real and that's really all that matters.

As for me, I have a very strong belief system—my years of ghost hunting have taught me that it's imperative to believe strongly in some type of divine power that can be called on for assistance.

I've seen and experienced too much not to know that there is something besides us out there in the universe. I guess the question you need to ask yourself is this: Do you believe, and if so, what do you believe in?

Now I'm sure there're those of you who would debate me until eternity about the existence of demons, and I'm sure you have some very good arguments. That's fine. Here's the deal: If the entities that can enter the world of the living and turn your life into a living hell to the point that they can actually possess people and take over their bodies aren't demons, then what are they?

I'm willing to concede the fact that "demons" might not be the appropriate word for what these phantoms are and what they can do, but until these specters can be identified as being anything but demons, then that's what we're going to go with, especially for the purposes of this book.

HOW DEMONS
GET HERE

Before someone can fully understand how demons oppress, re-press, infest, and possess, it's important to understand how demons behave, how they invade people's lives.

As with just about everything there are certain things that need to occur in order for a demon to fully enter your life and take over. There are those in the Christian faith who believe that God established rules of engagement that demons must adhere to and that these rules were put in place in an effort to protect us mere mortals from the forces of evil.

In my opinion this works in theory, but then again many things work in theory. But like some grand experiment on mankind, the rules have flaws—the main one being that God gave human beings free will, the freedom to choose. Part of being human means we're not perfect beings and therefore are prone to making wrong choices: hence, the ability for demons to infiltrate the world of the living.

Now, let's get down to the basics of how a demon can take up residence in our world.

A demon can't just enter your life. It must be invited or summoned in some way. In most cases the person unintentionally invites the demon into their lives. In a small amount of cases the person calls the demon in, summons the demon, or purposefully seeks them out.

For the purposes of this book, we are going to talk about the most prevalent ways a demon is brought into a person's life.

Séance and Ouija Board

One of the easiest ways for a demon to enter someone's life is if that person participates in séances or through the improper use of the Ouija board. Now, people who are experienced in handling a Ouija board and know how to protect themselves and others participating in a Ouija board session could walk away unscathed and/or untouched by a demonic entity. However, if you are relatively inexperienced you should not use a Ouija board or try to hold a séance at all. This should only be done in the presence of someone experienced with these tools who may be used to contacting the dead.

What séances and Ouija boards can do is open a door between the world of the living and the realm of the dead. In the paranormal community these doors are called portals. There's a controversy between paranormal researchers and mainstream scientists as to whether portals even exist.

Many paranormal investigators believe that portals can open and close to allow ghosts and spirits to travel from one location to another with relative ease and speed. Other paranormal researchers take it a step further and believe that portals act as gateways between the world of the living and the world of the dead. My belief is that both theories are possible.

Generally, mainstream scientists doubt the very existence of portals. Therefore, if they don't exist, then it would be impossible for a ghost or spirit of any kind to use them for travel. However, it's been my experience that many scientists don't believe in ghosts and/or spirits; therefore, the idea of spirit travel would seem absurd to them.

In response to mainstream scientists, many paranormal researchers argue that new discoveries are made in the field of science every year, so it's possible that our technology just hasn't caught up to what many people already know: Portals do exist and ghosts and spirits travel through them regularly, whether it's to get from one place to another or to go between the world of the living and the world of the dead.

Anyway, the inhabitants of the other side include but are not limited to spirits of the living that have passed, demons, and a myriad of other spectral beings that you don't even want to know about—at least not yet or in this book.

So when this door between the two worlds is opened, anything can come through it. Much like opening the door to your house—any man or beast can wander over the threshold. Whatever chooses to come through that door can be good or evil, light or dark, a human spirit or an inhuman spirit. The choice is not yours. The only choice that you have is that you make the decision to open the door. To a demon this may be all the invitation it needs to enter your life.

Just as with séances and Ouija boards, there's also the possibility that a mirror can act as a portal between the worlds of the living, the dead, and the inhumans.

For example, I had a case of a woman who was a very emotional person and almost constantly in a state of unrest over something. This woman loved to etch mirrors, which generally wouldn't be a problem, although personally I wouldn't recommend it because if you're like this woman, any emotions you're feeling at the time could be transferred into the mirror and open a portal.

Anyway, this woman and her family were experiencing frightening paranormal activity. She and her family were being pushed, shoved, and an unseen entity would grab them and try to drag them into the basement. The family moved from the house, but the woman took the mirror when they moved into the new home. The same type of activity occurred in their new residence.

It didn't take long to figure out that there were demonic forces at work in the house and that the origin of that activity was the mirror. Her negative emotions were enough to draw a demon through the mirror and into their home. Once the mirror was destroyed and out of the house, all paranormal activity stopped—a lesson for us all to be sure.

This is a case of what I would call a perfect paranormal storm. Now, to be sure, the house they found the mirror in was haunted, but it was haunted by a human spirit—not an inhuman spirit. The stress the family was under because of the haunting, coupled with the fact that the woman was a high-strung emotional wreck, led to all her emotions being transferred into the mirror when she started to etch it. When this happened, all those negative emotions were enough to lure a demonic entity through the mirror and into their lives.

By the time they moved, the demon had already chosen its target and was firmly ensconced in the mirror. Therefore it was easy for it to move with the family, since they took the mirror with them.

Appearing As Someone Else

It isn't uncommon for a demonic entity to appear as someone other than what it really is. For example, a demon could appear as a small child, your mother, father, grandparent, friend, or someone else you knew and trusted who is deceased. Even if the demon chooses to appear as a small child, we as humans wouldn't really think they are anything but what they seem to be. Let's face it, not many adults feel threatened by a child— even if that child is in spirit form.

The demon will do this because they want to gain your trust and, when you accept a child or a deceased loved one into your life, the demon takes that as an invitation to stay and take up residence in your home.

See, that's the point—because God gave humans free will we have to, at some level, consciously or unconsciously, intentionally or unintentionally, make the choice to let a demon into our lives.

Unintentional Contact

When you encounter a demon innocently or by accident, this is not an invitation to the demon and the demon can't harm you— at least not too seriously. I do have to say that in some respects a demonic entity will play "fair" when you first encounter it by giving you some type of warning. Not because they are being nice or "fair" but because God's law dictates the choice must be yours as to whether you engage or walk away.

Demons are extremely cunning creatures and when you first encounter them, they may imitate a normal haunting. In some cases you may hear footsteps, see shadows, have doors open and close, see lights turn on and off, etc.

For example, let's say you're ghost hunting, or just enter a space where you don't know a demon resides, and you encounter a demonic entity. The demon may react to your presence in one or more of the following ways: They may threaten you, growl at you, try to provoke you, physically push you or scratch you, mock your faith, or let you know in some other way as discussed above that they are there.

Once you know you're in the presence of a demon it's up to you to leave immediately, if not sooner. The demon has probably already given you a taste of its power, so now the choice is yours—to leave or to stay. If you choose to stay, you've made the choice to let the demon enter your life. That may not have been your intent, but to the demon your intent doesn't measure into the equation. Because you've made the choice to stay, the demon is then free to follow you home.

If you leave immediately the demon cannot follow you, harm your family or friends, or otherwise enter your life. You stumbled upon the demon unknowingly and unwillingly, and you have used your free will in choosing to leave and not engage the demonic entity in any way.

However, if you choose to return to that location knowing that there is possibly a demonic entity there, then you have pretty much sealed your fate—you have invited and accepted the demon into your life. Even after you leave again and decide to leave the demon alone, the fact that you chose to go back could cause the demon to follow you home and could be perceived by the demon as a form of acceptance into your life.

While these basic guidelines may seem too few for such vile creatures, the fact remains that they are really all that is needed. We either choose to engage in activities that could invite demons into our lives, or we don't. It's really just that simple.

It's important to point out that in some cases a demon may already be present when someone moves into a new home. While this may seem like an innocent encounter to you, and logic would dictate that it would be an unintentional encounter, it isn't—and this is why. You are willingly in its space. You didn't choose to leave despite the demon giving you ample warnings, even if you attribute the paranormal activity to a ghost or spirit that was once in human form. To the demon that could be construed as acceptance or an invitation, even if you don't know that what's causing your problems is a demonic entity.

For example, a case I worked on long ago involved a family that bought an old house. As is the case with many homes that have extreme paranormal activity, the former owners sold the home at a price that was almost too good to be true. There's a lesson there: If it seems too good to be true—it probably is.

Anyway, this family wasn't there long before the paranormal activity started, albeit slowly at first. They would hear scratching sounds that seemed to radiate from the walls, would catch something move out of the corner of their eyes, and they noticed that their dog would refuse to go down in the basement.

The husband called a critter service to see if perhaps bats, raccoons, or another type of small animal had taken up residence, which would account for the scratching noises. The exterminator searched the house from top to bottom and found no traces of any animals living in the home.

The homeowners then attributed the scratching noises to tree branches rubbing against the house when the wind would blow, so the husband cut the branches away from the home.

The activity not only persisted but became increasingly worse. Lights would turn on and off, doors would open and close on their own, and their four-year-old daughter started acting out in ways that were out of character for her.

When they asked their daughter why she was doing things she knew were wrong, she told them that a little boy who was in her room was telling her to do those things.

Becoming increasingly concerned, the parents contacted us. Once we heard about the activity occurring in the home, we flew into action, as we generally do when a child is involved. We told the family to arrange for the children and animals to be out of the house while we were conducting our investigation so if whatever was there retaliated, they wouldn't be harmed.

When we arrived at the house on a cold, rainy Saturday afternoon the first thing we noticed was that the air felt thick and heavy—almost oppressive. One of the team members commented that he felt as if he were trying to walk through peanut butter.

We spent about six or seven hours at the home conducting our investigation and captured some interesting EVPs. The one that sent chills up our spines was when we heard a gruff and menacing male voice tell us "The girl child will be mine."

Knowing that we were dealing with some type of negative entity, we became extremely concerned for the family's safety and knew we had to act fast to rid the home of the dark specter. After getting the owners out of the house, we got to work. I planned on using a ritual that combined binding, expulsion, cleansing, and blessing to get rid of the entity in the home.

I retrieved two boxes of Kosher sea salt, Holy Water, a smudge stick, and a cross from my car, and the team and I prepared to do battle. When I began the ritual, the energy in the house started to ramp up. It was as if the energy was swirling around us like the wind.

As we carried on with the ritual a dark shadow came out of nowhere and pushed me backwards against the wall. I knew this was its attempt to scare me and get me to stop what I was doing, but there was no chance of that happening.

I said the prayers as I carefully tied paper with words of binding and banishment on them around the smudge stick. As I set the stick on fire, the entire team started reciting prayers asking for help from God.

Once that was done we did a complete house clearing and blessing. As we worked we could feel the air become lighter. It felt as if a giant weight was lifted from our shoulders and we could breathe.

I left the family with instructions on how to bless and smudge their home and requested that they do this every week for the next three months and then every other week for a period of two months and then once a month going forward.

It's been over fifteen years since we visited that home and from what I hear, all is well. The children are grown and everyone is healthy and happy.

The example above serves to illustrate how demons take the guidelines set down by God literally, not figuratively, and demons don't make allowances for variables such as not knowing the paranormal activity was being caused by a demonic entity, or the fact that you may not personally believe in demons.

The important lesson to take away from this is that just because you don't believe in something, doesn't mean it doesn't exist, which is why it's important to keep an open mind at least to the possibility of demons actually existing—because I can assure you, they do.

Those who have fallen prey to a demon and have lived through a demonic haunting will probably tell you it was one of the most frightening experiences of their lives.

The sad fact is that those who have been preyed upon by a demon will probably not talk about it.

Because of the stigma that still exists in today's society regarding hauntings, demons, and other types of paranormal activity, many demonic hauntings go largely unreported. There are paranormal investigators, including myself, who believe that demonic hauntings may not be as rare as previously thought. Unfortunately this fact also plays into the hand of the demonic entity, because one of their main objectives is to isolate their victim from family and friends so that they can take control of their victim.

Negative Energy

Although rather rare, it's not beyond the scope of possibility for a demonic entity to be attracted to a certain location due to negative energy. Before getting into the details, let's look at negative energy in the broader sense of the term.

Because demons are negative entities, they are going to be attracted to negative energy—like energies attract.

Let me preface this next statement by saying that all energy, whether positive or negative, radiates out into the universe and the environment. Demons, ghosts, spirits, and some humans who are gifted in some way are capable of interpreting this energy and reacting in kind based upon whether that energy is negative or positive.

Negative energy is raw and unrefined; therefore it could be construed as being stronger than positive energy. When we, as humans, are happy or engaged in an activity that we enjoy, our energy is positive and on a pretty even keel. However, when we experience some type of anxiety or stress, this could cause our heart rates to rise, our blood pressure to rise, and our bodies to react in a physiological manner that is put out into the universe as negative energy.

There are many things that we as humans feel and do that can be construed as negative by a demon—remember, demons take things literally.

For example, if there is excessive alcohol or drug use in a home, this can weaken a living person physically and emotionally. Excessive drug or alcohol abuse are both negative activities and could produce enough negative energy to attract a demon.

In addition, domestic violence taking place in a family could attract a demon because of the negative actions and energy this type of activity emits into the universe. It's important to keep in mind that physical domestic abuse doesn't have to be present to attract a demonic entity; all it may take is frequent or constant arguing between spouses or between parent and child.

Also, demons thrive in chaotic environments and an unorderly home—one that is dirty, messy, and/or cluttered—may be all the invitation it takes in some cases. Now I'm not saying a home has to be hospital sanitary, but it should be neat and clean.

If someone in the home is an extremely emotional or high-strung person this could also lure a demon into a home. Emotional and high-strung people tend to concentrate on negative emotions such as sadness and/or excessive worrying. These types of people may cry, yell, be nervous, and almost always be in a state of upset over something real or imagined—in other words, drama queens or kings.

Ghost Hunting

As much as I hate to admit it, it's very possible that ghost hunting could allow a demonic entity into your life. As ghost hunters, any type of paranormal activity while investigating a location gets us excited. So we pull out our digital recorders and any other equipment we may have to eagerly make every attempt to interact in some way with the ghost or spirit that may be occupying the property. Before doing this, many ghost hunters don't stop and think about what type of entity they may be dealing with.

It's very easy to get caught up in the moment when you're ghost hunting or conducting paranormal research in a specific location. Because of the willingness to interact on the part of the ghost hunters, a demon could take this action as an invitation to enter one or more of the ghost hunters' lives.

There are certain precautions ghost hunters can take before they investigate any location. First, every paranormal investigator should educate themselves about what types of entities they may run into while on an investigation. They should read just about anything they can get their hands on about negative entities and demons.

Another thing every ghost hunter should do is come up with a personal protection plan against negative entities, whether they are human or inhuman beings.

For example, wear a cross or other amulet that you believe will offer you some form of protection based on your personal beliefs.

In addition, watch out for thoughts that enter your head that are not your own, or are urging you to do something that would be totally out of character. Pay attention to what you're physically feeling as well. When in the presence of a demon the air might feel particularly heavy or dense. It's possible it may be hard to breathe or to catch your breath. One might experience an overwhelming feeling of sadness, anger, and/or fear. Pay attention to these feelings and figure out if they're your own feelings, someone else's feelings, or if you're being oppressed, repressed, or influenced by a demonic entity.

While it may be possible for a negative entity to influence how you feel, the main difference is that with a demon, the emotions and physical symptoms you may feel will be more pronounced and stronger.

HOW DEMONS OPERATE

Once the demon has been invited into your life, either intentionally or unintentionally, there are certain things the demonic entity is going to do to gain your trust in order to take over your life. The demon is going to come at you from a lot of different directions and not all of them involve physical intimidation. However, that is among the most dangerous methods a demon has at their disposal.

It's important to remember when dealing with a demonic entity that this is the highest form of spiritual warfare that can possibly occur. Therefore, a demon is not going to hold back any weapon at its disposal to achieve its goal—which is to destroy its victim. So how exactly does a demon do that? Let's talk about the different types of warfare a demon is going to employ to infuse itself into your life and take over. Keep in mind the demon is going to fire all its guns at the same time, meaning that it's going to hit you with physical intimidation, psychological warfare, emotional torment, and try to isolate you all at the same time—there is not a checklist that the demon hits one by one.

The demon operates this way in order to keep you confused and off-balance—so you never know what's coming next and when.

Physical Intimidation

It's been my experience that demons don't always use physical violence or physical intimidation to the extent that's depicted in movies and on television. However, many times a demon will make itself known by using physical intimidation at the outset of a demonic haunting.

Demons can intimidate you by scratching, biting, pushing, and in some cases, attacking. Speaking from experience I can tell you that being attacked by a demon is something you never forget or recover from quickly.

A friend of mine, Leslie, was attacked by a demon three times while she was sleeping. She reported being held down in her bed, unable to scream or move. She could feel the hotness of the demon's breath on her face and the weight of its body on hers.

Now some skeptics may say she was a victim of sleep paralysis and in any other case I would consider that a valid argument. As noted before, sleep paralysis is a condition that can occur during sleep when the brain and the body aren't on the same page. In other words, you become mentally aware before your body wakes up and for a brief period of time a person will be unable to move or speak and may have hallucinations, most commonly of an evil presence either holding them down or in the room.

However, in this case it doesn't apply because Leslie had been in known contact with a demonic entity and she'd antagonized that demon on several occasions. In other words, she did everything wrong.

The last thing anyone should do is antagonize or engage a demon in any way. This is just asking for trouble. My friend, however, didn't know this at the time, and even if she had, I'm not sure it would have stopped her, as sometimes curiosity over-rules common sense.

When Leslie first came into contact with the demon she wasn't sure what type of entity she was dealing with—actually, the thought that she might have been dealing with a demon never crossed her mind. She did, however, believe that the entity may have been a negative spirit due to the heaviness in the air. She spent a lot of time at the location and would often try to verbally entice this entity into some type of paranormal behavior so she would have more information at her disposal to try to figure out what this entity wanted.

However, this entity started to go after Leslie's friends and not come at her directly. For example, friends that she'd taken past this location would report nightmares, or in some cases become ill shortly after being at the location.

This led Leslie to take matters into her own hands and confront the demon by telling it to leave her friends alone, and if it wanted to come after someone to come after her. As you can imagine, this was a huge mistake. The entity complied and this was when the physical attacks on Leslie began to take place. It was also when Leslie realized she was dealing with a demonic entity and not a normal ghost.

In my opinion, because there were no reported incidents of sleep paralysis occurring either before she had come in contact with the demon or after those three attacks, sleep paralysis was not the cause of these episodes.

One of the main reasons a demon will use physical violence or intimidation is to keep you in a state of fear because you will never know when the next attack is coming or how bad it will be.

At this stage it wouldn't be uncommon for a demon to hurt or kill one or more of your pets as well. While the demon may not choose to physically kill one of your animals, it's fully capable of it. Instead the demon may choose to make the animal so ill that it has to be euthanized or be kept at the veterinarian's office for treatment.

Cats, dogs, and other animals are very sensitive to ghosts, spirits, and demons. In my house my cats are my early warning system. They pick up an entity seconds before I do, but it's enough to give me a warning that something is in the house that shouldn't be.

By eliminating the animal, the demon is taking away any warning you may have, which to the demon leaves you more vulnerable to attack.

This is so the demon can wear you down physically, emotionally, and psychologically. Many people who are victims of physical demonic intimidation may not be getting enough sleep because they are under an enormous amount of stress due to the physical attacks.

Psychological Warfare

Demons are masters at psychological warfare and in my opinion it is one of their main weapons of choice. Depending on the demon, some type of physical intimidation was probably used to weaken you psychologically and now the demon can really get to work.

A demon knows your deepest and darkest fear and that's what it's going to target. How they know this information is still a mystery to me, but they do know—and they will use it against you.

Now I'm not talking a fear of spiders, dolls, clowns, snakes, or other superficial, illogical fears, I'm talking the deep-rooted, you've-never-told-anyone fear. It could be the fear of something happening to your family and friends, being abandoned, death, etc. What that fear is really isn't important. What is important is you have that fear and the demon can and will exploit it.

As an example, the same friend who was attacked by a demon in her sleep would take her friends by the house where the demon dwelled one by one if they asked to see it. She wouldn't take any of her friends into the house; she would simply drive by the home or pull into the driveway.

Within a week or so after being at the house, the friend she took there would experience something bad in their life. It could be a family member becoming very ill when they had been perfectly healthy, a relative getting into a horrible car accident, or some other tragedy. However, whatever the event was, it never happened to the friend, it always happened to someone that friend was close to. Coincidence? I don't believe in coincidences. It was the demon.

These events scared my friend so much that she quit taking anyone past the demon-infested house or talking about the demon to any of her friends or family. You see, my friend's greatest fear is something horrible happening to her friends and family. The demon knew this and played upon this fear in a huge way—psychological warfare.

Keep in mind this is just an example; it is not how a demon may use psychological warfare on someone else—it all depends on that person's deepest fear. The reason a demon will do this is to not only weaken their intended victim psychologically, but to isolate them.

The fact that my friend played into the demon's hands and didn't talk about it or take any people by the house where the demon dwelled was exactly what the demon wanted.

By using your deepest fear against you, the demon will effectively try to isolate you from your family and friends, thereby taking away your support system. At that point it's just you and the demon.

I believe one of the worst things about the type psychological warfare being waged by a demonic entity is that unless the intended victim knows what to look for, they won't even realize how they're being manipulated until it's too late and they are caught up in the demon's web. Think of a fly caught in the web of a spider and you'll begin to get the idea.

SIGNS OF A
DEMONIC INFESTATION

Most demons do not immediately possess a person—there are stages, or warnings, if you prefer, that lead up to full-blown demonic possession. They are infestation, repression, oppression, and possession. One should be careful to distinguish between them because each stage is markedly different.

It's important to note that you can have a demonic infestation, repression, and oppression and not have it turn into a demonic possession.

Generally, before repression, oppression, and/or possession occurs, a demonic entity will infest a location. There are specific signs of a demonic infestation or haunting, and many of them mimic an intelligent haunting of a spirit that was once in human form. This is why it's sometimes so difficult, even for seasoned paranormal investigators, to distinguish between a ghost or spirit and a demon. The following are what you need to watch out for.

Changes in Your Home

This is one of the signs of a traditional or intelligent haunting that could also be a demonic haunting. A person might have electrical or battery-operated appliances or gadgets that begin to operate on their own. For example, lights may turn on and off, children's toys that are battery-operated may turn on by themselves, the television may turn on or off and, in some cases, change channels.

In many cases electrical appliances, such as a blender, toaster, stove, etc., may begin to operate on their own. Some people have reported water faucets turning on.

A person may experience objects moving on their own or being thrown across a room. There have been reports of plates, cups, and glasses being hurled out of cabinets, dining room chairs being stacked, and other furniture being moved around a room, all without scientific explanation.

In some cases objects disappear completely or turn up in another location. Sometimes things such as coins or other small objects may seem to drop from the ceiling and come from nowhere.

Drawers and doors could open and close by themselves. Glass may break without a logical explanation or you might hear the sound of glass breaking but nothing is found to be amiss.

I worked on one case where a demonic entity was suspected and all the meat in the refrigerator and freezer would be fresh one day and be rotten and crawling with maggots the next. The service man was called out several times to make sure the refrigerator was operating normally, but nothing mechanical could be found wrong. At one point the refrigerator was replaced with a new one and the same thing kept happening. This activity by the demon is markedly different from a normal haunting and something only a demon could be capable of.

In addition, all the condiments or anything else in the refrigerator that was in liquid or semi-liquid form would be opened and appeared to have been thrown around the refrigerator. This person lived alone and no one else had keys, so there really was no logical explanation for what was happening.

Much of the activity that occurred in this specific home could have been written off as the work of a particularly nasty poltergeist; however, when coupled with the other activity that took place in this location, it could be attributed to nothing but a demon.

Noises

It's rather typical in a traditional or demonic infestation to hear unusual sounds that can't be attributed to natural causes—although I highly recommend seeking out a logical explanation before jumping to conclusions.

For example, people have reported hearing strange taps, raps, or banging on walls, doors, or windows. There have been reports of hearing a deep, throaty growl when no dogs are present, and other people have reported screeching, screaming, as well as disembodied voices.

Yet others have heard the sound of something heavy being dropped on a floor or the sound of furniture being dragged across a room, and when they go to investigate they discover nothing out of place or disturbed.

You may hear someone call out your name when there is no one else in the house, or you think someone in the house called to you but they didn't. This is generally not typical haunting behavior by a ghost, although it's not unheard of. For example, a deceased loved one may call your name to get your attention.

The same could be said for a demon; however, the intent with a demon is to frighten you. It's also possible for a demon to imitate the voice of your deceased family member or friend in order for you to be more accepting of its presence.

In addition, it would be pretty common to experience the sound of scratching or banging on walls and/or doors.

Again, this could be written off as typical poltergeist activity, which is why it's important to look at all the paranormal activity in the location as well as how the behavior of the living people in the home may have changed since the activity started.

Smells

Quite frequently in a traditional haunting, smells such as cigarette or cigar smoke, or the smell of perfume, may be experienced. In the case of a demonic infestation the odors will normally be markedly different.

It's typical in the presence of a demonic entity to smell a foul odor such as sulfur or rotting meat. The odors that may accompany a demonic infestation have been described by many as being a "stench," "bitter," or "very unusual."

Once you've had a whiff of an odor produced by a demon you will never forget it and may be hard pressed to describe it to someone or duplicate the exact smell. It's kind of a combination of rotting meat, sulfur, and rotten eggs—that's about as close as I can come to describing it.

Once when I was working a case in a home known to be occupied by a demon, I came in contact with the most unpleasant aroma I'd ever smelled. It was so strong and so intense it made my eyes water. Being that I was in the basement of an abandoned home that was well over a hundred years old, I thought perhaps an animal had died and the smell was coming from a decomposing carcass.

A complete search of every square inch of the basement and house turned up nothing, yet the smell lingered in the air and permeated not only my clothing, but what seemed like every pore of my body. Once I left the house the smell was completely gone.

Changes in the Air

A home or place of business that is experiencing a demonic infestation will generally experience a change in the feel of the air. The air in the building may feel "heavy" or "oppressive."

Some people I have personally worked with who were the victims of a demonic infestation have reported feeling like a weight was on their shoulders or they felt like they were having trouble breathing because of the heaviness in the air.

This change in the atmosphere of a location can be so extreme that when the demonic entity is gone the air feels lighter, the location brighter, and a huge sense of peace, calm, and relief floods the building.

My team and I encountered this type of energy once when investigating a home—it was not the first time and certainly would not be the last—but this time was slightly different in that the entire team felt it.

Some on the team described it as feeling as if someone's hands were pressing down on their shoulders, weighing them down; others said they felt a strong pressure in their head. Still others claimed that it felt hard to breathe and move, like they were moving in slow motion.

Sometimes the heaviness in the air can affect people's moods. They may feel melancholy, depressed, stressed, and/or anxious. These symptoms wouldn't be unusual when encountering an atmosphere of this type. It should be said that upon leaving the location, all of the symptoms disappeared.

Emotional Changes

People who have come into direct contact with a demon could experience changes in their moods and emotions. Demons feed off of negative energy, so the changes in someone's emotions or mood generally will not be positive.

For example, people may be prone to angry outbursts, act out aggressively, become depressed, or become apathetic to things and people around them.

These emotional changes will have a marked effect on their personal lives and the person may begin to lash out at friends and family, swear a blue streak when it is totally out of character for them, or completely withdraw and become highly anti-social.

Our team is very careful to note changes in moods and thoughts when they enter a location that is housing a possible negative energy. They watch out for thoughts that are not their own, and whether their actions are being influenced by someone other than themselves.

Physical Complications

Individuals who reside in a home with a demonic infestation could experience a wide variety of physical symptoms or illnesses that cannot be linked to a specific ailment.

As an example, a person might have unexplained bruises or scratches. Some people may experience nosebleeds, vomiting, vertigo, headaches, and other types of physiological conditions for which the medical profession is not able to find a logical explanation.

Having sleep issues could be a factor if a demonic entity is present in the home. Many paranormal investigators attribute this to the fact that demons appear to be more active during the nighttime hours than during the day—although demons are fully capable of acting out during the daylight hours as well.

There's a long-standing theory among many people in the paranormal community that demons are more active between midnight and 3:00 a.m., also referred to as "Dead Time." This is the time that many paranormal researchers believe ghosts are more active. However, with demons it may be for a different reason. It's generally accepted that many demons are most active at 3:00 a.m., because Jesus died at 3:00 p.m.; therefore, 3:00 a.m. would be the negative equivalent.

A person may experience unbelievably horrific nightmares that will disrupt their sleep. People are more vulnerable when they are in a sleep state because generally their natural defenses are down. A demon is well aware of this fact and will take advantage without hesitation.

There are paranormal investigators who believe that the peak time for a demon to be active is between 3:00 and 3:30 a.m. So it may not be unusual for a person to wake up during this time without knowing why they woke up. In some cases a person may wake up feeling that they've gotten enough rest, yet still feeling tired as if they didn't sleep at all. In other cases, a person may become so frightened by the signs of a demonic oppression that they are unable to sleep soundly—or in extreme cases, only sleep a minimal amount of hours per night.

As you can imagine, sleep deprivation can lead to a whole multitude of other symptoms, such as irritability, moodiness, inability to focus on a task at hand, etc.

A demon may cause sleep deprivation in its intended victim to wear them down physically and emotionally to make their victim more vulnerable to their influence and make their prey easier to control.

Physical Harm

Demonic entities can be very violent in nature and won't hesitate to attack. Besides the scratching and bruising that can take place, victims of a demon have reported having their hair pulled, or having been pushed or pulled to the point that they have fallen and become injured—sometimes seriously, especially if a flight of stairs is involved.

There have also been reports of welts showing up on people whose lives have been infiltrated by a demonic entity. It would also be likely that one could suffer from horrific attacks while sleeping. These attacks, as discussed earlier, can mimic sleep paralysis.

Changes in Animal Behavior

One of the main signs of a demonic entity is when your pets, especially a cat or dog, start to display behavior that is erratic or uncharacteristic.

The different behaviors that could be exhibited include withdrawing from the family and, in some cases, hiding, barking at something no one else can see, acting aggressively, displaying fright, or in the case of a cat, hissing or puffing all its hair out and taking a defensive posture.

Demons have been known to kill animals by either making them sick, or outright murdering them. So if you think you may have a demonic presence in your home it may be a good idea to leave your pets with friends or relatives until you get the issue resolved.

In my career as a ghost hunter I've seen horses refuse to go into a haunted barn, dogs and cats refuse to enter homes or certain rooms in the home, and dogs chase orbs.

While sometimes it is just a human spirit or ghost playing with an animal, if any animal begins to act afraid of its surroundings without a logical explanation, we would be wise to take notice and investigate further.

Becoming Withdrawn

Generally a demon will target one person in the home as their victim. This can occur during a demonic infestation. The infestation can lead to repression and then possession unless something is done to stop the demon from reaching that point.

The targeted individual may start to withdraw and lose interest in activities. It's possible the victim will start to miss school or work, and generally withdraw from previously enjoyed social and family functions.

Sometimes this type of behavior is caused by the demon starting the repression or possession process, but oftentimes this behavior is due to the victim becoming so frightened about their paranormal experiences that they don't want to share what's going on with others, so they keep the signs of the demonic haunting to themselves.

Unfortunately, in many societies, the United States included, there is still enough social stigma that a person who claims to be suffering from paranormal activity is afraid of being ridiculed, thought to be crazy, or ostracized from their peer groups, which can include their friends and co-workers.

By withdrawing from family and friends they are actually playing right into the demon's hands; one of the demon's main goals is to isolate their victim to gain control over them.

In some cases a demon will target a child or teenager because they are more open to the paranormal and extremely vulnerable. This is especially true if the child suffers from mood swings and/ or depression. A child that suffers from autism or another type of illness may also be considered a prime target for a demon. I'm not giving you this information to scare you; it's to help protect you and your children. Forewarned is forearmed when it comes to a demon.

If you notice someone in your family or one of your friends displaying this type of behavior it would be a good idea to sit down with them one-on-one and find out what's really going on in their lives—the answer may surprise you and it's up to you to be open to whatever they share with you. Perception is reality—it may not be your reality, but it's theirs, so be understanding and supportive.

If you suspect you or one of your family members are experiencing a demonic infestation, you should seek help from a paranormal professional or a member of clergy who has experience dealing with demonic entities.

DEMONIC
POSSESSION

When people hear the term "demonic possession" or that a person is "possessed," all kind of images may come to mind. If you've seen the movie *The Exorcist*, you may think of a young girl who has turned practically green with her head spinning completely around—which is impossible, by the way. Some might think of the scene when she was projectile vomiting all over the priest and anything else that happened to be in her way.

Whatever images come into your mind when you hear those terms, thanks to movies, television, and other media outlets, they are probably not correct.

Before we talk about demonic possession I feel that it's important to understand the difference between demonic oppression and demonic possession.

In demonic oppression the demon is influencing a person's behavior and their life, but the demon is not in control of their victim's mind and body.

In demonic possession the demon has gained full control of their victim's mind and body. The victim will quickly adopt the personality, voice, and actions of the demonic entity. No longer will the person be able to control their body or have free will, free consciousness, or freedom—they are totally under the control of the demon.

Demonic Repression

While the term "demonic repression" is not very well-known and is not used a lot in paranormal circles, it's still important to mention for the purposes of this book because it is very real.

Demonic repression involves the power of suggestion. The demon will come to a person, generally when they're asleep, and speak to them. When we are asleep we are more vulnerable to this type of activity and the demon will choose a victim they deem to be weak-minded or easily swayed by the power of suggestion. There will be a marked and profound effect on the life of the person who falls prey to demonic repression.

The reason the early warning sign of a demonic presence is in the form of repression is because the demon exerts its influence while their victim is asleep. This could lead most people to believe that they only had a dream or nightmare and more than likely dismiss it.

While this is a logical conclusion, it may not always be the correct one. That's why it's so important to understand all the signs of a demonic repression. If some of this type of activity is in conjunction with what is perceived to be a dream or nightmare, it could be something different altogether—a demonic repression.

The main symptom of demonic repression is that the victim will display radical thought patterns that are not in their normal character. This person may become argumentative and take a position that is profoundly different from what you know to be their normal views.

It's important to note that not all people who have become the victim of a demon will display signs of repression, as each demon operates just a little differently. In addition, the differences in personality, emotional temperament, and psychological stability of the victim all can play a role in whether or not that person will become demonically repressed.

For example, if the person is a very emotional person it may be easier for the demon to oppress that person and skip repression altogether. If the intended victim is stronger emotionally and psychologically than the demon first thought, then the demon might employ repression techniques to wear the person down before moving onto the oppression stage. In other words, because every living person is different, the demon can and will adjust their methods accordingly.

Demonic Oppression

Strictly speaking, demonic oppression is defined as being influenced mildly or heavily by a demon. Depending on who you talk to, it can also be the body's physical, emotional, and psychological response to the influence of a demon. In my opinion, it's a combination of both. If you're being influenced by a demon, your body and mind are going to respond in some fashion.

Anyone can fall victim to a demonic oppression, but generally people who surround themselves with a high level of negative people, thoughts, and behavior are more apt to experience a demonic oppression.

There are many signs that someone is being oppressed by a demonic entity and some of them can mimic a demonic infestation. For purposes of this book, I will not repeat those symptoms, so please refer back to the demonic infestation chapter.

Emotional

In some cases of demonic oppression the person may experience feelings of extreme anger, sadness, hopelessness, depression, or other negative emotions for which there is not a rational cause. They may also feel and display signs of high anxiety with no apparent reason or cause. In extreme cases the victim may entertain thoughts of suicide because they feel life is not worth living and believe they have no purpose.

Most of these symptoms of emotional distress can also be attributed to several mental and physical illnesses. Don't just jump to the conclusion that you or someone you know is being demonically repressed, but instead insist on a physical and psychological examination by qualified medical professionals.

Fear

It would be quite typical for the victim of a demonic oppression to feel an abnormal and extreme amount of fear that to friends and family might seem totally irrational and unfounded. However, in many cases, the person being oppressed knows something bad is happening to them but either can't or won't verbalize it.

A person experiencing this amount of fear may be scared of something specific or they could be experiencing fear in general. Either way, the fear may seem irrational to outsiders.

The amount of fear someone is feeling may be hard to discern at times because it could be the person is a normally private person, or they are fearful of things by nature. Therefore it may be up to you, whether you are a friend or family member, to draw that person out and get them to open up about what has them so afraid.

Look for non-verbal clues, meaning body language that could indicate someone is fearful. These include: breaking out in a cold sweat, avoiding eye contact, speech errors, voice tremors, or tension in their muscles, such as clenched hands, crossed legs, and being fidgety.

Conflict

The victim of a demonic oppression could begin to feel as if they are in an almost constant state of conflict both with themselves or others. A person could be argumentative in that they will pick fights, or take an opposing view just to argue.

They could also seem to be unable to make simple decisions.

Lack of Self-Control

A victim could feel and/or exhibit a total lack of self-control. They may feel an extreme amount of hatred and lash out verbally or physically at friends and loved ones.

Thought Complications

It's quite common for a victim of demonic oppression to have an inability to concentrate and have negative and/or destructive thoughts. This person may also experience thoughts that appear to come from somewhere else and that they recognize they are not their own, yet feel powerless to stop.

Loneliness

Even when surrounded by family and friends that they would normally enjoy, a victim may feel extreme and irrational loneliness—like they don't belong or are on the outside looking in. Look for people in this situation to withdraw from family and friends at social gatherings when it's normally out of character for them.

Substance Abuse

The victim may begin consuming alcohol heavily or begin to use drugs all in an attempt to escape the fear, anxiety, and other symptoms of a demonic oppression.

Hedonism

Hedonism is the almost relentless pursuit of entertainment or bodily pleasure. For example a person suffering from demonic oppression may become promiscuous when they were sexually conservative before. They could form an addiction to pornography where none previously existed.

Escapism

Many times a victim will try to escape the terror of what's happening to them by forming an addiction to thrill-seeking, video games, or any other type of hobby or activity that can be addictive and allow them the opportunity to escape.

Keep in mind that some people have addictive personalities and quickly jump from one obsession to another. However, a person who hasn't displayed an addictive personality in the past and suddenly starts to do so should be cause for concern and be investigated.

Demonic repression and oppression are possible stages a demon will use while on their way to possessing a person. It is possible to stop the demon at these stages before the situation escalates into a full-blown demonic possession.

The Difference Between
Spirit Attachment and Possession

It's important to understand the difference between a spirit attachment and demonic possession, because there are marked differences.

First, a spirit that attaches itself to a living person is generally not a demon. It can be any one of many types of spirit that roam the universe. They are kind of like leeches: They attach to the living in order to use that person's energy.

These types of spirits will feed slowly over a period of time until the host becomes so weak they get very sick and eventually may die if something is not done to remove the spirit. In some extreme cases, when the living person gets into an extremely weakened state, they are ripe for possession.

A demonic possession is a totally different ballgame. A demon isn't going to wait around or have the patience for what can be the extremely slow process of attachment. A demon is going to find a way to breech someone's free will to get inside a person's body and take control unless someone or something steps in to stop it.

Possession

People becoming possessed by demons happens more often than many people realize but is still considered extremely rare in both religious and paranormal circles. However, before such illnesses as schizophrenia, Tourette's syndrome, and a host of other physical and mental illnesses were discovered, people who had these diseases were thought to be possessed and were often subjected to horrific exorcisms that did more harm than good—and sometimes resulted in death.

Many people even today use such cases of misdiagnosed illnesses as proof that demons don't exist, and that therefore it would be impossible to be possessed by one.

The truth is that science doesn't have all the answers and is constantly changing as new discoveries are made. In addition, some very specific and unexplainable manifestations can take place during a demonic possession that cannot be explained by science.

According to the Spiritual Research Foundation, in the current era until 2025, thirty percent of the population will be possessed by demons and/or other negative energies. That would mean that for every ten people who read this book, three are possessed, five are affected by them, and two will be unaffected.

Personally I'm not sure I agree with their stance, as the numbers seem a little high. However, if their research is correct and their numbers are right, the prospects for the future as far as demonic possession is concerned is bleak, to say the least.

As I said before, there was terrible treatment in the past of people who had a mental or physical illness, and those people were demonized. What generally happens when religion and science come together is that things can go too far. In some cases, mentally ill patients are being given antipsychotic drugs and practically turned into zombies. In recent years things have gotten better for mentally ill patients, but what about for people who are actually possessed? In some cases they are treated as being mentally ill and literally being treated for a disease or illness that they aren't suffering from.

It should be said that some people who are mentally ill are possessed. Now the question becomes: Are they possessed because they are mentally ill or are they mentally ill because they're possessed?

There really isn't an easy answer to that question, but there are clues. When someone is possessed there are so many different events going on around them, called "outward manifestations," that a person would be hard-pressed to say that what is going on is strictly a mental illness.

There are a lot of changes occurring in and around a person who is truly possessed by a demon and they fall into three categories: outward manifestations, physical changes, and mental changes. We're going to break them down one by one. Keep in mind that not every person who is possessed is going to suffer from or experience all of the symptoms in every category.

Outward Manifestations

In order to not be repetitive, I'll ask you to please look to the section on demonic hauntings for other outward manifestations that aren't mentioned here. The same thing will occur during a possession, but they could become amplified and increase dramatically—kind of like a demonic haunting on steroids. Other outward manifestations are listed here:

Religious Articles

Religious items such as crosses, bibles, statues of saints, angels, etc. may disappear or be completely destroyed. This could also occur during a demonic haunting.

In the case of a demonic possession, the possessed individual could have a strong negative reaction to religious items and may be unable to recite even the simplest of prayers.

Lights, Shadows, and Creatures

It wouldn't be unusual to experience strange lights darting around the house, a particular room, or around the person who is being possessed. Sometimes the activity may only occur when the victim is present or the activity may seem to revolve around them.

Dark shadows or people may be seen and these shadows may or may not have a distinct form, such as the shape of a creature or person. Although rare, it's possible that strange or scary creatures may be seen, generally out of the corner of your eye. If you do see one of these creatures or dark shadows, I can tell you from personal experience it makes you question your own sanity.

I've seen two creatures in my thirty-plus years of ghost hunting that to this day have me shaking my head. The first was a bona fide demon—the second I'm still trying to figure out.

I saw the demon one night when I was coming back from a ghost hunt. I decided to swing past an abandoned mansion just outside of town on my way home. I pulled into the dirt driveway and glanced up at the side of the large house, which was illuminated by an outside light atop a pole next to the home. I thought I saw some kind of distortion in the bricks between the two second-floor bedroom windows, but dismissed it as being caused by the way the light was hitting that portion of the house.

I could feel energy radiating out from the house and it became stronger as I walked closer. It felt thick, heavy, and decidedly menacing. It became so strong that it was making me nauseous—my personal warning sign that a negative spirit was close by. I leaned against a large tree waiting for the wave of nausea to pass and as I did so I glanced up at the house.

From between the two windows on the second floor I saw a beast emerge. The head was wolf-like and the arms resembled dragon's feet, for lack of a better description. They were claw-like with long talons. The eyes of the beast were red with pure black pupils and they were staring right at me.

It took only a split second to realize I was in real danger, and given that it was two o'clock in the morning and I was extremely tired, I didn't need to be told twice to get out of there. I scurried back to my car and went home.

I saw the other creature when our team was called in to investigate a church. The main part of the church dated back into the late 1800s but additions in the few years preceding our arrival more than doubled the size. A church cemetery sat across the parking lot.

The old part of the church contained the chapel area and a large steeple. We'd concluded our ghost hunt, and while several spirits were present, they weren't a threat; in fact, they were two old caretakers who were still looking after the church after death. They both were buried in the church cemetery.

The only thing I would consider out of the ordinary was that when I was up in the balcony of the chapel area, I saw a door that, when opened, led to an extremely small storage closet. Looking up, I could see all the way to the top of the steeple. When I walked by that door during my initial sweep of the building, I heard something growl at me from behind that door. It startled me enough to make me recoil away from it.

One of the investigators I was with heard it as well and when he opened the door there was nothing there.

It was well after 2:00 a.m. when I walked to my car to leave. As I drove out of the parking lot I looked towards the church and saw that lights illuminated the steeple. As I glanced at the steeple I could swear I saw an impish creature clinging to the side of it. The creature looked elfish with a small body, and oversized head, hands, and feet. It was basically almost hairless, and its face was football-shaped. It gave me an evil grin when it realized I was staring at it.

To this day I can't be sure I actually saw this creature or if it was my mind playing tricks on me due to the lateness of the hour.

Temperature Changes and Fire

Just as in a demonic haunting, the temperature in a particular room may drop or increase—although normally the temperature will decrease dramatically. Many paranormal investigators speculate that when the temperature drops noticeably something paranormal is about to occur.

The theory is that an entity needs energy to manifest or create some type of disturbance so the entity will literally suck the energy out of the room or feed on the energy in the space, which would explain the decrease in temperature.

In the case of a demonic haunting or possession, spontaneous fires may start anywhere in the house.

Cold spots or drops in temperature in a home or room don't necessarily mean a demonic entity is present. This type of activity can occur in the case of a traditional haunting where the only culprit is a normal spirit. In many cases it turns out the coldness is caused by a draft, so it's important to look for logical explanations for any type of activity you may be experiencing.

Strange Sensations

Someone who is being subjected to possession or a demonic haunting may feel gusts of wind blowing at them or in a room even when all the windows and doors are closed.

A person may feel like they are being watched or they are not alone. The person may also experience movement out of the corner of their eye that may or may not accompany these feelings.

Before jumping to conclusions, I would have an electrician come into the home and make sure there is not an extraordinarily high electromagnetic energy field (EMF) in the home, and if there is, repair the electrical system to get the electromagnetic energy back to the normal range. In the paranormal community, a high EMF can cause what is known as a fear cage.

If a person is in a fear cage, they may experience the feeling of being watched, touched, and a general creepy feeling—like they're not alone. Many times these feelings are attributed to paranormal activity when in reality there's a logical explanation.

Levitation

Yes, just like in the movies and on television, it is possible for a demonic entity to levitate objects and people. The objects could be as large as a bed or couch, and as small as a pin. It's not the object that really matters, it's the fact that it was levitated at all that is cause for concern.

It's also possible for ghosts and spirits to move or levitate some objects, so don't jump to conclusions that it's a demonic entity causing the activity. Although, if people are being levi-tated, it's a good bet you're dealing with something negative.

Sexual Assaults

Demons and demonic entities such as incubi and succubi are very capable of sexually assaulting their victim. The assault could range from fondling to full penetration. A sexual assault by a de-mon can happen to both men and women and are generally at-tributed to the incubus and succubus types of demons.

Retaliation

Any attempt to rid the home of the demonic entity or to help the person who is possessed could lead to swift and extreme re-taliation on the part of the demon. The retaliation will be an in-crease in activity that could include physical and sexual assaults on the part of the demon.

There could be retaliation after a member of the clergy or a paranormal investigator has been brought in, and it could in-crease dramatically if someone attempts to say prayers.

Sometimes it seems as if the demon knows someone is com-ing to make an attempt to get rid of it. In some cases, I have gone as far as to tell my clients not to discuss the activity in the home, or disclose the fact that a paranormal team or member of clergy is going to be paying a visit. I do this because I know it's possible for the entity to react negatively and the safety of my clients could be at risk. It may also be wise to tell your clients to leave the home and stay in a hotel or with family and friends until the problem is resolved.

However, this isn't always effective because demons have been known to follow people anywhere they go. If the entity does follow someone, especially if one of the family members is possessed, the demon could be angry and lash out viciously, causing even more harm than if the family had stayed in the home. It's a tightrope and not an easy call to make. One has to weigh the pros and cons before recommending this to anyone.

Psychological Changes

The psychological changes that occur in demonic oppression and repression also apply to the psychological changes that can occur during a possession, along with the following:

Changes in Attitude

An extroverted person may suddenly become introverted and isolate themselves from their family, friends, and co-workers.

A person may begin to curse a lot, which would be completely out of character for them.

The possessed person may become hostile and argumentative over little things that normally wouldn't bother them or for no apparent reason at all. The victim could become abusive, threatening, or violent. In the case of violence, it wouldn't be unusual for them to attempt to hurt or kill animals.

A person who once went to church may no longer attend or may show repulsion at the thought. This person may also start destroying religious objects and mocking their and others' religion.

Changes in Habits

The possessed person could experience weight loss or weight gain and experience changes in their sleep patterns—nightmares and night terrors wouldn't be uncommon.

They may start to indulge in self-mutilation, like cutting themselves.

A person who is possessed may drastically change how they dress and there could be a marked difference in their personal hygiene habits.

A victim of possession may change their eating habits, such as forming a sudden aversion to foods that were once their favorites and starting to eat foods they hated.

It wouldn't be out of the ordinary for the possessed person to perform humiliating acts such as urinating on themselves.

They may also become sexually obsessed and start masturbating in front of others or privately. They could also form a fascination with pornography to the point of obsession.

Multiple Personalities

A person who is possessed may start to display symptoms of multiple personalities and have blackouts and not remember anything that happened when the other personality or personalities took over.

Keep in mind this is also a sign of a mental illness and the person should be taken to a psychiatrist to determine whether they have multiple-personality disorder or their symptoms are due to something else entirely, such as demonic possession.

Psychic Changes

Someone possessed by a demonic entity may exhibit signs of precognition, which is the ability to predict the future.

They may also show signs of retro cognition, which is the ability to know about events that took place in the past that they would normally have no prior knowledge of.

The victim of a demonic possession could know something about a person they just met that they would have no way of knowing.

In some cases, the possessed individual may be able to read your thoughts and know exactly what you're thinking.

Physical Changes

There are many physical changes that can take place during a possession. Some of them are more subtle than others, but they are changes just the same.

Language

A possessed person may start to speak in a voice that is not their own. They might start speaking their native language with strange accents or speak in a different language that they didn't know before the possession took place. It's also possible that the possessed person may start to speak in tongues.

Their voice may change and become very deep or very high. Generally speaking, a guttural voice would be more common in a possession situation, but demons can manifest themselves in whichever way they choose.

It's also not out of the realm of possibility that multiple voices may come from the possessed person at the same time.

Changes in Features

A person who is possessed will probably show distinct changes in their features. Pay special attention to their eyes: they may change color. More than likely they will turn black, almost like shark eyes.

This person could also appear catatonic. Keep in mind this is also a symptom of a mental illness or a neurological problem and it should be checked out by a qualified physician immediately.

A person's hair color may also change dramatically. It could go from dark to light or vice versa. In some cases their hair could turn shocking white or gray almost overnight.

Other Physical Changes

The victim of a possession may have superhuman strength and be able to lift heavy furniture and throw it across the room as if it were as light as a feather.

Their walk may change and it could appear as if they were almost "gliding" across the floor instead of taking actual footsteps.

Some possessed people become completely rigid and cannot be moved at all, even by multiple people.

Writing and/or symbols could appear on a possessed person's body in the form of welts or scratches. Pay attention to these occurrences—especially where it would be impossible for the possessed person to reach by themselves.

One of the first warnings that a person is possessed or is becoming possessed is if animals are frightened by the person or avoid them altogether when they normally wouldn't.

Levels of Demonic Possession

There are those who believe that there are three levels of demonic possession: mild, medium, and severe. Some of these people or groups categorize the degree of possession based on the level of sixth sense or perceptive ability that would be required by an outsider to identify another person as being possessed.

While I may not necessarily agree with these people and, in some respects, I find their methods flawed, this is still important information and one of my goals with this book is to present all points of view, whether I agree with them or not.

Mild Demonic Possession

In the case of mild possession, almost anyone should be able to notice something is different or unusual about the person. For example, there would be marked changes in their personality and behavior. The person who is possessed may become hostile or aggressive, laugh hysterically, or talk in a different language.

Some people believe that a person who is only mildly possessed is being possessed by a lower-level demon or a ghost. They believe that the ghost or demon is only out to harm the person.

While I agree that there are different levels of demons— meaning some are more powerful than others—to me, a demon is a demon and it's got to go. While I personally have not encountered a person possessed by a ghost or a ghost that can possess, it's not out of the realm of possibility. To me, if it's a ghost or a type of spirit other than a demon, it's more likely to be a case of spirit attachment rather than possession.

Medium Possession

According to some people, when a medium becomes possessed it is very subtle. It would require a person with a rather heightened level of sixth sense to be able to tell if a medium is possessed.

A person who tries to calm down a medium-possessed person would have some difficulty in calming the person completely down. Also in a medium possession the ghost would have to be a higher-level type of spirit and would only have fifty percent control over the person they are possessing.

Many of these people believe that this type of ghost would be a female goblin or a medium-level ghost. The goal of the possessing spirit would be to have some influence over the individual and to affect society in some way.

Severe Possession

The people who believe in the theory of different levels of possession believe that if a person is severely possessed, only a saint would have the ability to detect the possession.

They also believe that during a severe possession the demon has roughly seventy-five percent control over a person. They also believe that the goal of the possessing spirit is much more sinister and would involve nationwide destruction and have a detrimental effect on the world as a whole.

As an example, they believe that Hitler was possessed by a subtle sorcerer from the lower regions of hell.

The Possession Syndrome

The possession syndrome is characterized by something demonic having full control of a person's mind; however, the demon is not real but is simply a projection of the human mind. In other words, the person truly believes they are possessed.

People who suffer from the possession syndrome are suffering from paranormal distress in which they believe they are being controlled by a demon, spirit, alien, or in some cases, God.

The possession syndrome exists around the world and has been reported by many people. Psychologists believe this condition exists mostly in people with little education, a low social status, young females, people who are divorced, and in a few cases, newly recruited members of the armed forces.

Many psychologists also believe that childhood abuse, neglect, loneliness, isolation, and emotionally, socially, or psychologically distressing experiences could be at the root of causing the possession syndrome.

The possession syndrome is also a known disease and medically meets the criteria of having specific symptoms and clinical findings; however, there isn't any recognizable lab or imaging evidence that can verify a diagnosis. In some cases, people claiming to be suffering from the possession syndrome are hoaxes.

In addition, because a lot of psychiatrists aren't comfortable with the term "possession," they are labeling it as obsessive-compulsive disorder, multiple-personality disorder, dissociative identity disorder, or intermittent explosive disorder.

The main problem with the possession syndrome is that psychotherapy cannot adequately treat this disease and in some cases an exorcism is the only way a patient can find relief from their symptoms.

Some psychologists and psychiatrists have a theory that when a person is faced with mounting stress they enter a possession-trance to resolve the conflict. In addition, while the person is "possessed" they can release repressed impulses and anger, which in turn could alleviate the feelings of anxiety and tension the person is experiencing.

Other symptoms of the possession syndrome can include headaches, vomiting, abdominal pain, blindness, epileptic-type seizures,or hallucinations; abnormal walking, talking, or facial expressions; emotional instability; and antisocial, violent, and/or homicidal behaviors.

Symptoms that would appear to be paranormal in nature could include but aren't limited to: talking in another language, knowledge the person normally couldn't have, supernatural strength, and being able to manipulate objects and themselves without explanation.

People suffering from the possession syndrome sometimes need more than prescribed medication and psychotherapy. These patients need support to get them through this frightening, disorientating, and spiritual crisis. They need a type of spiritual psychotherapist who will ask the right questions when these patients have lost their belief in God and have rejected organized religions. They need something spiritual to believe in. It's important to remember that people who are suffering from the possession syndrome truly believe that they are being possessed by another being or entity. Remember—perception is reality. It may not be our reality, but for the person who is suffering the most, whether real or imagined, it is their reality.

I believe that sometimes psychologists and other mental health professionals have to operate inside their patient's reality and outside of their own reality in order to best serve the patient.

The problem with the possession syndrome is that some people use this as an excuse, or to escape having to take responsibility for the most despicable acts they have done to others.

As an example, take the case of Andrea Yates, the woman who drowned her five children in 2001. Ms. Yates was completely convinced that she was possessed by Satan, which compelled her to commit such a heinous act.

Was she possessed? That's up for debate. Was she suffering from the possession syndrome? Completely possible. Or are Ms. Yates and her defense team using the possession syndrome or demonic possession as a legal defense? We will probably never know for sure.

In the not-too-distant future it's possible that the possession syndrome could cause a slippery slope in the fields of psychology and law. The question for psychologists and psychiatrists is whether or not they can set aside prescribing medication and psychotherapy and open themselves to the possibility that the possession syndrome does exist, and sometimes they may have to look at an exorcism to help their patients who are suffering from the possession syndrome.

In the field of law, the courts are going to have to look at the possession syndrome with fresh eyes. They are going to have to determine if the possession syndrome is a viable defense for certain crimes and if so, what are the options for punishment for those crimes? The courts and juries are going to have to decide if the person claiming to suffer from the possession syndrome is telling the truth or simply using it as an excuse.

The hard part for the fields of psychology and law is going to be separating those people who are legitimately suffering from the possession syndrome from those who are simply trying to perpetuate a hoax, or those who are truly demonically possessed.

Possession Syndrome or Mental Illness

It seems like more and more when you turn on the news you hear about someone being murdered because either the person who committed the murder thought they were possessed or they thought the person they killed was possessed.

Even David Berkowitz, aka the "Son of Sam" killer, claimed that while he wasn't possessed, the neighbor's dog was and it was the possessed dog that ordered him to kill all those people. He later amended his statement, claiming that he'd been part of a Satanic cult and the killings were part of a ritual.

The real question is: Is demonic possession being used as an excuse, or do those people truly believe they or their victim(s) are possessed?

First Demonic Possession Used As a Defense

Dubbed the "Demon Murder Trial" by the media, the case of Sam Brock was the first known case in the United States in which an attorney used demonic possession as a defense, in this case for his client's brutal murder of his landlord.

The attorney argued that Mr. Brock had a long history of erratic behavior and his parents had even been in contact with various demonologists throughout Mr. Brock's childhood. The attorney also argued that Mr. Brock didn't murder his landlord because he was mentally ill, but because he was possessed by a demonic entity.

The judge in the case didn't buy the argument and ruled that demonic possession was not a valid defense against first-degree murder charges. Mr. Brock was convicted but served less than half of his ten- to twenty-year sentence.

Murder in a Small Town

The police were alerted to possible trouble when a man's ex-wife called and asked the police to do a welfare check on her son after his father was late bringing him back from his visitation.

When the police arrived at the home, the man said his son wasn't there and that he (the man) was a Boy Scout leader and a good person. Becoming suspicious, the police forced their way into the home and made a grisly discovery that rocked even the most seasoned officer to his very core.

The father admitted to hacking his teenage son to death with an ax, claiming that his son was a demon. The father further asserted that he was afraid his demon son was going to eat him.

Upon further investigation, the police learned from the neighbors that the man was considered "odd." All the windows were covered in tinfoil and none of the neighbors recalled seeing the young man outside playing when he was visiting his father. Neighbors also reported that the man had jumped out of the bushes at some of the women and the police had been called to the man's house numerous times over the previous few weeks.

The boy's father tried to wrestle away from the police and screamed about war and other things as he was being led away to jail.

Possessed Pastor?

Charles Zenith went to the home of a local pastor hoping the man could pray with him. For the last few months, Charles had been tormented by voices in his head telling him to do horrible things.

The next morning, one of the neighbors heard strange noises coming from the pastor's basement apartment and found the pastor lying on the floor, unresponsive. The neighbor immediately called the police.

Upon arriving at the home, the police noticed Charles pacing and jumping at the front door. As the police approached, Charles disappeared into the home with the police in pursuit. Charles broke out a window with his bare hands and was apprehended trying to crawl out of the broken window.

As soon as the police found the pastor's body, Charles began yelling that he killed the demon and that he kills demons. While it wasn't quite clear what exactly happened in the pastor's apartment, Charles was charged with first-degree murder in the asphyxiation death of the pastor.

Murder Most Foul

For Toby Cox, his alleged demonic possession began after he cheated on his wife with a woman from their church. Toby claimed he felt as if a terrible evil was welling up inside of him that he had no control over. This feeling became so strong he violently attacked his lover.

After a series of strange behaviors, Toby went to his church for help in dealing with the evil that grew inside him. A group of priests met at Toby's home to perform an exorcism.

For well over twenty-four hours the priests worked tirelessly to rid Toby of the demons. Finally, in a state of total exhaustion, the priests stopped and declared they'd rid Toby's body of at least forty demons, but warned him that there was still a lot of evil inside of him.

Toby was back to normal for only a short time before the police department found him outside his house, totally naked and covered in blood. When the police entered the house they found that Toby had brutally murdered his wife by ripping out her tongue and eyes and tearing half the woman's face off. They also found that Toby had killed the family dog; however, the dog was only strangled, not mutilated.

Much to the town's dismay, Toby was acquitted of all charges by reason of insanity. However, Toby showed up in future news stories. He has attempted suicide on several occasions and was recently put on trial for child molestation.

Molestation—Excuse or Demon Possession?

A young man named Noah went on a missionary trip to a small country in Africa. While there he molested a number of the children that he'd been sent to help.

Text messages Noah sent to friends during his stay in Africa show that Noah believed he was possessed by a demon he named "David" that forced him to commit these sexually explicit acts on the children. Noah claimed that, "What David wanted—David got."

Noah's text messages also revealed that he was horrified by the creature he felt was residing inside his body, but he felt powerless to stop it, and had no idea how to control it or get rid of it. He tried desperately to pray the demon away, but it wouldn't leave him.

Now, Noah faces life in prison for the heinous acts he committed while in Africa. A federal judge ordered that Noah be kept in jail until the time of his trial, claiming that Noah is a danger to the community. This decision overturned a lower court's ruling that Noah be released into the custody of his parents and must reside at the family home.

Noah's attorney, however, tells a different tale altogether. He claims that authorities in Africa confined Noah to a small room and wouldn't give him food, water, or his passport until he wrote down his confession to the crimes. The African authorities allegedly held Noah for four or five days and coerced the confession under duress.

The attorney further alleges that it was the African authorities that planted the idea of demonic possession inside Noah's head and even told him that he should call the demon "David."

There's a lot going on with this case, and it's just a matter of what you choose to believe. It's entirely possible that Noah was being influenced by a demon to commit these crimes against the children, but it's equally as possible that Noah is using that as an excuse, or for some reason the African authorities are making him a scapegoat to cover up another person's crimes.

Whatever the truth is, Noah could spend the rest of his life in prison and those children will have to deal with the emotional and psychological scars of the sexual abuse they suffered for the rest of their lives.

As in so many of the cases in this book, people tend to lose sight of the real victims and concentrate on the perpetrators all because they were either possessed, or believed the person(s) they killed were possessed. Yet in other cases it just seems like an excuse to commit cold-blooded murder or other heinous crimes.

EXORCISMS

While in most societies exorcism is thought of as being a ritual for driving demons out of a person, place, or thing, technically it's making the demon swear to an oath. The very word "exorcism" comes from the Greek preposition "ek" with the verb "horkizo," which means "I cause to swear." This means the demon is being forced to swear to an oath or the person performing the exorcism is invoking a higher power to bind the demon or negative entity so it can be controlled and made to act against its own will.

To put it bluntly, the exorcist is doing to the demon what the demon did to the person it decided to possess—control and force it to act upon the possessed person's free will. Don't you love it when karma works so efficiently?

Many people associate exorcisms with the Roman Catholic Church when in reality, the Protestants, Pentecostals, and other religions practice exorcism as well. However, in other religions an exorcism may be referred to as "deliverance ministry."

In deliverance ministry, the pastor or another gifted person drives the demon out by putting their hands on the possessed person. This is called "laying on of hands" and "praying" over them.

There are many lines of thought on exorcisms in society, and what it boils down to is either you believe it or you don't—the choice of whether to believe or not lies with every individual person. For the purposes of this book I will generally stick with the Roman Catholic Church's exorcism rites and rituals.

History of Exorcism

During the early days of Christianity—from the second century onwards—exorcism was a popular term, and there is little doubt that the practice of exorcism is very ancient and is comprised of several belief systems and different cultures and religions.

By the end of the third century and into the early fourteenth century the church noticed some abuses taking place when it came to exorcism, so they took steps to end the problems.

In order to have a system within the church, the church started the Ordained Order of Exorcists. This took place at the 4th Council of Carthage in 398 A.D. Out of this council 104 canons were formed, and Canon 7 dealt specifically with exorcisms.

When the exorcist was officially ordained, they received a small book that contained the written rite of exorcism. The exorcist was instructed to memorize the prayers. They would then have the power and be able to lay hands on people who were demonically possessed. The book the exorcists were given is no longer in existence in any written form and has been lost to time.

Over the next millennium items were added to the rite of exorcism as the church saw fit. One of the most significant changes was that instead of just using the name of Jesus, certain passages from the Holy Scripture officially became part of the Rites.

The use of Holy Water, exaltation, and breathing on the possessed person were added over a period of over one thousand years.

In 1614, the first standardized version of the Rites of Exorcism appeared in the Rituale Romano. This version cautioned priests not to perform exorcisms on people who weren't truly possessed. However, with the advancement of medicine and psychology, determining who is truly possessed and who is suffering from a mental illness or neurosis makes this task increasingly difficult. Only very minor changes were made to this version between 1614 and the Second Vatican Council, which occurred between 1962 and 1965.

In the mid-1900s, some revisions were made to the wording that involved the symptoms of possession, from "are signs of the presence of a demon" to "might be." One of the other changes was from "those who suffer from melancholia or any other illness" to "those who suffer from illness, particularly mental illness."

These changes can be attributed to the fact that between the years of 1960 and 1980, psychology and Western reasoning seemed to replace religion and spirituality. It was almost as if demons didn't exist anymore and exorcisms were thought by many to be a superstition in the church. Be that as it may, just because someone doesn't believe in something, doesn't mean it doesn't exist and isn't just lying in wait, getting ready to strike.

In 1998, the Rites of Exorcism were revised yet again and released in 1999. There were a few changes, some of which many priests don't agree with. The minor change was the fact that the

Rite was being printed in English and not the native language of the church—Latin.

However, some priests within the church have a few problems with the revised Rites issued in 1999. Some object to the use of the word "asks" in the sentence, "When the Church asks publicly and authoritatively in the name of Jesus Christ that a person or object be protected against the power of the Evil One and withdrawn from his domain, it is called exorcism." The objection is that the sentence seems to imply that an exorcism is now a prayer to God. Some priests feel this language is too passive because they believe an exorcism is not a prayer to God but a command to the demon to vacate the person or premises.

In addition, these new Rites give a priest a choice between two forms of exorcism, which the rites call "deprecatory" and "imperative." Deprecatory is a prayer to God, while imperative is a command to the demon to leave in the name of God. While the difference is subtle, it is there. Some priests believe that a deprecatory isn't an exorcism at all, but a request to God to intervene. These priests believe that the imperative version is a true exorcism. They argue that simply putting the heading of "Exorcism" over the deprecatory version doesn't make it an exorcism.

Further, the 1999 Rites specifically state that the priest must always use the deprecatory version and that the use of the imperative version of the rites is used at the discretion of the priest—in other words, it's optional.

Also, the Rites of Exorcism of 1614 contained twenty-one directives that gave the exorcists guidance about how to proceed with an exorcism. The revised Rites only have nine directives—

twelve of the original twenty-one directives were omitted from the 1999 Rites of Exorcism and weren't replaced or updated in the 1999 directives.

I've paraphrased the deleted directives and they are as follows in the order they first appeared:

4. In order to better understand demons and possession, the priest should ask the person who was possessed what they experienced while they were possessed and while the exorcism is being performed. The priest should pay special attention to the words that the victim reports had a negative effect on the demon so that these words may be used more frequently in future possessions.

Basically what they're asking is that the church-sanctioned exorcists collect as much data as possible in regards to what specific words or phrases seemed to have an effect on the possessing demon.

By gathering this information, the church could compile these different words and circulate them to all the exorcists. This could enable the exorcists to incorporate these words and phrases frequently in future exorcisms and speed up the process of getting the demonic entities to leave their victims' bodies faster than before.

5. The priest should be on guard for tricks that a demon may use in an effort to deceive the exorcist. Frequently demons lie and try to confuse the exorcist. This is done in an effort to make the priest get tired or give up. The

demon may also try to fool the exorcist into thinking they've left the body of their victim when they really haven't so the exorcist will stop the exorcism.

Even though demons were never alive in human form, they do have a strong sense of survival. If they feel that they are losing the spiritual warfare battle and will be forced to leave the body of their victim, they will pull out all stops to remain with their victim.

At other times they will try to deceive the exorcist through lies and other methods in an effort to have the exorcist become so exhausted that they give up and stop the exorcism.

The church wanted exorcists to be aware of all possible tricks and attempts at deception a demon will try in an effort to make the exorcism stop.

6. Quite often the demon will try to hide themselves so the victim believes they are rid of the possessing demon. However, the priest shouldn't stop until they see signs of deliverance.

Demons may try to fool the exorcist by hiding and have the victim appear to be perfectly normal so that the exorcist will stop the exorcism and leave the demon in peace. This directive was originally put into place to warn the exorcist of this fact so that they won't stop the exorcism until all signs of the demon are completely gone.

8. Sometimes the demon may reveal what the church perceives as a crime, such as witchcraft that has been commit-

ted, and the person who committed the act that caused the person to be possessed. They do this in an attempt to end the exorcism. However, the priest should not resort to superstitions or any type of forbidden practice.

Clearly this directive was important and valid in the 1600s and probably up through most of the 1800s; however, there really isn't a need for it now and it should have been removed from the revised directive, as it deals with witchcraft and the fact that a church-appointed exorcist should not resort to witchcraft or any other activity that is not sanctioned by the Church while performing an exorcism.

9. There are times when the demon will leave the victim in peace and let them participate in the holy Eucharist to make the victim think the demon has departed. Many times this is an act of deception on the part of the demon and the priest should not fall victim to such a trap.

This directive refers to the fact that a demon is capable of hiding in an attempt to trick the exorcist into stopping the exorcism because the demon wants the exorcist to believe they've left their victim.

Clearly this directive was covered in previous directives and should have been removed. The only problem I can see is that most of the other directives that refer to this have also been removed.

13. The priest should have a crucifix in his hand or in sight of the possessed victim. If any relics of the saints

are available they should be applied to the breast and head of the victim after they have been properly encased and covered. The priest must make sure these religious objects are not mishandled and that no harm comes to them by the demon.

This directive deals with the proper placement of religious symbols, such as a crucifix, on the possessed person's body. It also gives exorcists the precautionary warning that the religious symbols should not be damaged in any way or otherwise defiled by the demon.

14. The exorcist should not try to carry on a conversation with the demon or ask any questions about the future or any hidden matters. Rather, the exorcist will order the demon to remain quiet and speak only to answer a question that is asked. The exorcist should not acknowledge the demon if he later states that he is the spirit of a saint, a deceased person, or claims to be a heavenly angel.

This directive instructs the exorcist not to quiz the demon about any future events or any secretive or hidden matters. It also directs the exorcist not to engage in conversation with the demon, but to order the demon to be quiet and not to speak to the exorcist unless it is answering a question posed to it by the exorcist.

It also warns the exorcist not to believe or respond to a demon that professes to be a deceased saint, a deceased person, or an angel from heaven.

Because demons are infamous for pretending to be something or someone they're not, this is a valid directive and in my opinion should have remained in the current version of the Rites of Exorcism.

> 15. There are, however, some necessary questions the exorcist should try to obtain answers to. They include: the time they entered their victim, the reason they entered the victim, etc. If the demon begins laughing, talking nonsense, or taunting the exorcist, the exorcist should try to prevent it, or order the demon to stop. The exorcist should also order any assistants or observers, of which there should be very few, to ignore such babblings of the demon and forbid the observers from asking any questions of the demon.

This directive instructs the exorcist to try to get answers from the demon on how long it's possessed the victim and what caused it to choose the possessed person as a target.

It also instructs the exorcist to stop any incessant babbling, taunting, or laughing by the demon at this stage of the exorcism. It also informs the exorcist that their assistants or anyone else present shouldn't acknowledge such behavior from the demon either.

> 16. The priest should say the Rites of Exorcism in a commanding voice and with authority. At the same time the exorcist should be exuding a lot of confidence, humility, and fervor. When the exorcist sees that the demon is becoming upset, he should oppress and threaten it even more.

This directive urges the exorcist to speak in a firm voice and with confidence when addressing the demon and performing the Rites of Exorcism. It also tells the exorcist that when the demon shows signs of being stressed or any form of distress, the exorcist should double his efforts and threaten the demon even more than they already have. In doing this, the exorcist may force the demon out of the possessed person's body in a shorter amount of time and with less stress on the victim.

In my opinion this is crucial advice and should have been included in the current Rites of Exorcism.

> 17. The exorcist should pay close attention to what words and phrases cause the demon to become agitated or up-set and repeat them more frequently. When the priest comes to a particularly threatening statement, he should repeat it over and over to increase the punishment to the demon. If the exorcist believes he is making progress, he should continue for two, three, or four hours, or longer if possible, until the demon is driven out.

This directive tells the exorcist to pay close attention to what words and phrases seems to affect the demon the most and to use those specific words more frequently. It also directs the exorcist to continue the exorcism for as long as possible once those key words or phrases are discovered in order to force the demon out of the victim's body.

This directive is much like another directive already mentioned. The problem is that the other directive addressing this issue was also removed from the current exorcism rites.

19. If the priest is performing an exorcism of a woman, he should always have other women present to hold the possessed woman down when she is being tormented by the demon. The assistants should be relatives of the possessed woman for decency purposes and the exorcist will avoid saying or doing anything that might cause him to have evil thoughts.

This directive was designed to protect not only the exorcist but the victim. It directs the exorcist to have female assistants, preferably relatives of the possessed person, if that person happened to be a woman. The job of the female assistants would be to hold the possessed woman down if she was being tormented by the demon.

This directive was specifically put into place to ensure that the priest wouldn't be accused of taking advantage of the possessed woman and that the woman was safe.

In my opinion, this directive would still apply today and should have remained in the current Rites.

20. While performing the exorcism, the priest should use only the words from the Holy Writ and not his own or those of someone else. The exorcist should command the demon to tell him if it has been put into the victim's body due to an act of sorcery or magic. The priest should also inquire as to whether the possessed person has ingested items of magic, and if so, they should vomit them up to rid the body of these items. If the items in question are outside of the possessed person's body, those objects

should be found and burned. The possessed person should also be made to confess all his temptations.

This directive instructs the exorcist to use only the words in the Rites and not to improvise with their own words. It also instructs the priest to quiz the demon about whether its victim had eaten or swallowed anything that had to do with magic or sorcery, and if so, the exorcist should attempt to have the victim vomit these items up so they could be properly destroyed.

In addition, the exorcist should force the possessed person to confess all their sins and temptations so that their soul could be cleansed.

It's clear that this directive was outdated and probably should have been removed from the revised rites.

The priests who perform exorcisms claim that the above directives, which were used for over 385 years, were crucial directives in performing exorcisms and should have been included or revised in whatever way necessary in the 1999 Rites of Exorcism; they should not have been eliminated altogether.

Discussion of the 1999 Rites of Exorcism

As one reads through the directives that have been deleted, it becomes increasingly clear that the meat and potatoes have been taken out of the directives as they pertain to the Rites of Exorcism.

The omitted directives provided clear-cut guidance to the exorcist for almost any situation that may arise. The current directives, while important, don't contain all the fortification that an exorcist clearly needs when doing battle with a demon.

Now the argument could be made that most exorcists are very experienced and know exactly what to do and how to conduct a proper and successful exorcism. I can accept that argument and it goes a long way to explain why in the last few years there has been a return to the ancient prayers by Church exorcists. However, the official reason isn't clear.

My concern is with the new or less-experienced exorcists sent out by the Church to perform their duty. They have little to go on and, in addition, they don't even have to perform the "true exorcism" if they choose not to, as discussed above.

So the question for me is: Do the Rites of Exorcism of 1999 diminish the effectiveness or chances of survival for a person who is truly possessed? Naturally, an experienced exorcist should know to use the true exorcism, and not just the deprecatory version. An exorcist with enough experience more than likely will take the proper steps to ensure not only his safety, but the safety of his assistants and the person who is possessed.

It just seems to me that taking some of the most important directives out of the 1999 Rites of Exorcism, when a priest and the victim of possession are in the middle of one of the highest forms of spiritual warfare possible, is not a prudent decision and these directives should be revisited and returned to the Rites of Exorcism the next time it is revised.

In addition, if a priest decides to only use the deprecatory Rite that asks God to intervene, it may not be effective in ridding the possessed person of a demon. Some are of the opinion that the Church has inadvertently put possessed people in possible danger due to the fact that the real exorcism is optional, and these people believe that the imperative Rites of Exorcism should be made mandatory.

Again, an experienced exorcist is either going to include the imperative Rites of Exorcism or is going to use the old version to ensure that the demon has left its victim and the person is no longer possessed.

Another question that concerns me is: If an exorcist only uses the deprecatory version, is he putting himself and his assistants in harm's way? Remember, this Rite only requests that God intervene to rectify the situation; it does not command the demon to leave.

I'm not saying that the exorcist would intentionally put anyone in danger. However, one of the biggest risks an exorcist faces during an exorcism is that the demon may leave its victim and possess the exorcist or one of their assistants. It seems to many that by not making the imperative Rites of Exorcism mandatory, the Church allows unnecessary risks to be taken.

The Directives Contained in the 1999 Rites of Exorcism

The nine directives that remain in the Rites of Exorcism, and again I've paraphrased, are as follows:

1. A priest who is authorized to perform an exorcism on a possessed person should be distinguished for his piety, prudence, and integrity. He should be humble and rely not on his own power but on the power of the divine. He should be of mature age and revered not just for his office as priest, but for his high morals.

2. To do his job as an exorcist properly, he should study the exorcisms performed by others, paying special attention to the important points that occurred during those exorcisms.

3. The exorcist should not believe too hastily that a person is truly possessed by a demon, but should look for signs that the person is suffering from some other type of illness—especially an illness that is psychological. The signs of possession could be: the ability to speak and/or understand a foreign language, the ability to know the future and/or hidden events, showing that they have powers that are beyond the victim's age and knowledge, and other signs that when put together build up evidence for possession.

4. The demon may place whatever obstructions they are capable of in an attempt to keep the victim from getting an exorcism, or the demon may try to convince their victim that what they are experiencing is a natural condition. Further, during the exorcism, the demon may cause the victim to fall asleep or put up some illusion while the demon itself hides so that its victim seems to be rid of the demon.

5. The exorcist will always be mindful of the Lord's words that there are certain types of demons or evil spirits that cannot be made to leave except by prayers and fasting. The priest should say prayers and fast before he attempts an exorcism and encourage his assistants and the victim to do the same.

6. If possible, the possessed person should be moved to a church or other sacred place for the exorcism and away from a lot of people. However, if the possessed person

is ill or has any other valid reason, the exorcism can be
performed in their home.

7. The possessed person, if in good mental and physical health, should be instructed to ask for God's help,
fast, and take holy communion as often as possible or
at the discretion of the priest. The victim should also be
instructed that during the exorcism they are to focus on
God, and to never doubt divine assistance.

8. The exorcist should refrain from giving the possessed
person any type of medicine and should leave that decision up to the victim's doctors.

9. After the exorcism has concluded and the victim is
freed of the demon, they should be instructed about not
giving in to sin, to reduce the chances of the evil spirit
returning and making the victim worse than he was the
first time he was possessed.

The one thing that is pleasing to see is that the new Rites of
Exorcism contain an exorcism for a place or thing, not just a person. However, the exorcism for a place or thing still requires the
permission of the bishop before a priest can use it. In addition,
the choice to use the imperative exorcism is still at the exorcist's
discretion and is not required by the Church.

In my opinion, it's about time the Church lent some guidance
on the proper procedures and prayers for exorcising a building or
object.

Many priests expect that one day the Rites of Exorcism will again be revised and the hope is that the directives will be reworked and expanded upon, along with making the imperative Rite mandatory and not a matter of choice.

Exorcism in Modern Society

With the advances in science and psychology, many people turned their backs on the belief in demons, and some even decried religion as being nothing but mythology. Exorcisms in the Roman Catholic Church and other religions were still conducted by the very faithful, but out of sight of the ridiculing eyes of mainstream society.

In the not-so-distant past even the mention of religious doctrine would be met with a pitiful stare and questions as to why someone still believed in such things as demons, angels, and God. In many cases, Christians were too meek and timid to stand up for what they believed in, especially if they felt peer pressure or felt outnumbered—after all, no one likes to be harassed because of their beliefs.

This movement away from organized religion by modern society alarmed many in the Church, as it should. To them it seemed that God was falling out of favor and the devil was finally getting his due.

Many people of other religious beliefs became increasingly alarmed as well. There are those, myself included, who believe that all things in the universe must remain in balance. This can include but isn't limited to light and dark, good and evil, etc.

With the decline of many in society following any personal religious beliefs at all, the balance in the universe could be upset, with the scales leaning more toward evil or darkness and straying away from the light and goodness. If anyone watches the evening news it's not hard to see that the power struggle between good and evil is askew.

While many light workers around the world are feverishly doing whatever they can to return the universe to balance, the Roman Catholic Church has recently taken some steps to protect society from demonic entities.

For example, the International Association of Exorcists, which was founded in 1992, is bringing some continuity, in regard to terms and practice, to the exorcist community. In addition, this organization is fostering networking and mentoring practices among exorcists—something that didn't exist before.

The Vatican itself is getting involved by holding an annual course on Exorcism and Prayers of Liberation. This step is going a long way in making huge strides in the training of new exorcists, and bringing the existence of demonic evil into the forefront of not only the Church but society.

The United States Conference of Catholic Bishops is attempting to create a pastoral directory of exorcists in the United States that would help new exorcists and define certain terms that would be universal.

In my opinion, what would help is if the Church acknowledged that there may be some people who could be trained to perform exorcisms who aren't priests or involved with the Catholic Church. I realize that the likeliness of this happening anytime soon is very slim, but maybe if paranormal teams and the Church worked together more consistently, a lot more could be accomplished in dealing with demonic entities.

I did recently read that the Vatican is offering classes on demonology not only to priests but to lay people. This is certainly a giant step and substantial progress by the Church—which I hope continues to expand and grow in the future.

There are a lot of people in the paranormal community who are not connected with the Roman Catholic Church and many of them, myself included, are on the front lines of what's going on when it comes to paranormal activity and the presence of a possible demon. Many of these people also believe in God, Jesus, or some other Higher Power(s) to turn to in times of need. But some of these people have a problem with organized religions and are not only very "religious" but spiritual, and give more of their lives to their beliefs than some of the people involved in organized religions.

This is not to say that there's anything wrong with organized religion, because there's not. Spiritual beliefs are a matter of personal choice and one shouldn't be condemned for what one chooses to believe, unless those beliefs interfere with the right to religious and spiritual freedom of others.

I will say that with the new Pope, the Church appears to be changing in some ways to keep up with the times. I can only hope that those changes include more open views when it comes to the paranormal and non–Roman Catholics being trained in the Rites of Exorcism.

There are those individuals outside of the Church and, in many cases, organized religions, who perform exorcisms. They may call themselves demonologists, exorcists, or both. There are also those who profess to be exorcists who aren't and take advantage of people who are in a terrifying situation. Many of these predators are really con artists who scam people out of money.

As an example, there was a priest in Florence a few years back who would put on shows for an organization he founded close to where he lived. This priest would get a dozen or so of his friends or fellow priests to pretend they were possessed so he could free them of Satan and rake in donations from the people who attended these shows. It took many years to catch this priest and he'd managed to get donations to the tune of almost five million dollars before being apprehended.

How Is an Exorcist Chosen in the Roman Catholic Church?

Being an exorcist is not something everyone can or should do, or even aspire to be. Those who are exorcists view what they do as a calling from God. These people have a faith and belief in God and Christianity that is unwavering and steadfast. To put it simply, they cannot be tempted to abandon their spiritual beliefs.

The Roman Catholic Church looks at five areas of a priest's life in order to determine if he can be mandated to perform an exorcism.

Devoutness

This is a measure of the priest's faithfulness to God and the Church. Has the priest shown that he performs his duties to God and the Church in a devout manner? The answer to this question must be yes in the eyes of the Church and the diocese bishop.

Knowledge

A priest who is mandated to do an exorcism must have wisdom and the ability to think clearly and be a deep thinker. The priest must have an understanding of life through life experiences.

Discipline

An exorcist should act on reason, not emotion, and show good judgment.

Integrity

The priest must have high morals and always do the right thing, even if no one is looking. He must be above reproach and not be able to be corrupted.

Training

Not every priest can perform an exorcism or call themselves an exorcist. They must be trained in demonology, possession, and exorcism, and know how to recognize demonic influence. They also must be able to look at the possible demonic attack from a physical and psychological point of view.

The exorcist must be as free from sin as humanly possible in the eyes of the Church because the greatest danger to an exorcist is becoming possessed by the demon they're trying to exorcise. If the exorcist harbors a secret that needs to be punished, it makes it easier for the demon to entrap and possess them.

Different Types of Exorcisms

In the Roman Catholic Church, there are two types of exorcisms available: Simple, also referred to as a Minor exorcism, and a Real or Major exorcism.

Minor Exorcism

In the Roman Catholic Church, a Minor exorcism is what some Christians call a baptism. The Solemn Rite of Exorcism is not used in a Minor exorcism, but a different Rite is used. It is used on someone who is becoming a Catholic, and on a person who isn't possessed but is thought to be under the dominion of a demon because they haven't been baptized.

There are other Christian religions that use prayers to "deliver" someone from the hands of demons. In some cases the "laying on of hands" or "praying over" someone who is believed to be possessed could be considered a Simple exorcism.

Major Exorcism

In a Major exorcism, the Rites of Exorcism are used to assist a living person in getting rid of a demon that has possessed them. This is normally the type of exorcism that comes to people's minds when they hear a reference to an exorcism.

A former Jesuit professor, Malachi Martin, said in his book *Hostage to the Devil* (1976) that an exorcism can succeed or fail based upon who is performing the exorcism.

Martin goes on to say that an exorcism should occur in a place that is familiar or has a connection to both the demon and the victim, such as the victim's bedroom or home.

It's very rare that an exorcist will work alone. Generally they have two assistants—one being a junior priest who is trained in the Rites of Exorcism. This assistant normally will monitor the exorcism and help the exorcist during the procedure to ensure he is not distracted by the demon. The other assistant can be a physician or a member of the family of the possessed.

There are those who believe that an exorcism is broken down into specific stages: the Presence, Breakpoint, Voice, Clash, and Expulsion.

The Presence

During this phase, the exorcist becomes aware of the presence of the demon. Generally the victim will appear to be making attempts or actions of evil intent when in reality it's the demonic entity controlling the victim. This is when the exorcist will attempt to find out what entity they're dealing with by attempting to get the demon to reveal its name.

The Breakpoint

This is the moment when the demon gives up its name. It's also generally the point when all holy hell breaks loose and pandemonium reigns. Panic, confusion, abuse, horrible sights, noises, and horrendous odors will all occur. The demon will then turn on the victim and could start talking about them in the third person.

The Voice

This is one of the main signs of the breakpoint. The voice of the demon may become quite disturbing, and distressing language and verbiage may spew from the victim's mouth using the demon's voice.

In order for the exorcism to proceed, the exorcist needs to silence this voice.

The Clash

As the voices subside they will be replaced by a spiritual and physical pressure. The demon has collided with the forces of good and the exorcist is in a direct spiritual battle with the demon. The exorcist may choose to use this time to extract more information from the demon in order to be able to control it.

Some people believe that the demon needs a place to be or it must return to hell. If this is true, then the demon is actually fighting to remain out of hell.

The Expulsion

This is the final act as the demon leaves the victim in the name of Jesus and succumbs to God's will. This may be accompanied by a feeling of euphoria. The air may seem lighter, the residence brighter, and a kind of calm will fall upon all concerned. Many people have reported feeling as if a weight has been lifted off of them and they feel less burdened or oppressed.

During the exorcism the priest will wear his surplice (a white robe) and purple stole. Sometimes the surplice is adorned with lace a few inches above the edge of the hem or sleeves. The surplice is intended to represent an alb, which is the symbol of the white piece of clothing worn at a Baptism. The ritual itself is a series of prayers, appeals, and statements said at different times throughout the exorcism. At specific times during the exorcism the priest may sprinkle everyone in the room with Holy Water, put his hands on the victim, make the sign of the cross on himself and the possessed person, and may touch the victim with a cross or other religious item. When the exorcism is completed, the victim may or may not remember anything that has happened.

The Issues with the Exorcism Process

The main problem facing the Roman Catholic Church and paranormal investigators that deal specifically with dark entities is maintaining the balance between credulity and incredulity.

By that I mean the people who believe demons are everywhere and those who believe demons and/or other dark entities don't exist at all. Unfortunately the latter has infiltrated the Church to some extent and some people who need help aren't getting it and are being pushed away. This is due to the fact that our society has become so materialistic that many people now view paranormal matters and believing in demons to be a matter of superstition, backward thinking, or as antiquated mythology.

However, there are issues when a person's claim of demonic activity is true and the process they have to go through before receiving much-needed assistance could serve to make the problem worse, or in some cases, help may arrive too late.

Here's why: When you go to the Church for help, they do a very extensive investigation to ensure the person isn't suffering from a psychological disorder, on drugs (both legal and illegal), or outright lying.

This investigation can take weeks or months to complete and, depending on who is doing the investigation, it may be possible that the Church goes too far in one direction.

Once the investigation is completed, all the evidence is then taken to the bishop, who can take it under advisement to review the case. If the bishop deems that the Solemn Rite of Exorcism needs to be performed, he will then appoint a mandated exorcist. Again, this could take a rather long period of time.

Personally I have no problem with conducting a complete investigation of someone claiming to be under the influence of a demon. This is a very necessary step. However, the length of time a formal investigation by the Church can take leaves someone who has a legitimate case out in the cold and by themselves to battle the demonic entity on their own until the proper channels are gone through with the Church.

Another problem that can arise is that the person being affected by the demon may not take the issue to their priest or other member of clergy out of embarrassment or the fear that someone they know may deem them to be crazy. I'm not saying a member of clergy would call this person crazy, but that may be the perception of the victim under a demonic influence.

These people are more likely to contact a paranormal investigator before going to their church for assistance. Herein lies the real problem.

It's entirely possible for a skilled paranormal investigator to complete the investigation in a relatively short period of time. If the investigator is pretty sure there is a dark entity or a demonic entity present, under the laws of the Church there's really nothing more the paranormal investigator can do.

This is why more paranormal investigators are networking to find people who can help with demonic entities. There are various other religions besides the Catholic Church capable of performing exorcisms and that have people within those religions who are expertly trained to deal with such situations. It can't be stated strongly enough that paranormal investigators have no business undertaking the exorcism of a possessed person—that is best left up to the Church and their corps of properly trained exorcists.

The solution would be for the Church and paranormal investigators to work together to help as many people who are legitimately being plagued by demonic entities as possible, so they can get the proper help faster and more efficiently.

Another problem that the Church faces when it comes to exorcisms is that many in the hierarchy of the Roman Catholic

Church don't believe in ghosts. Instead they believe that a ghost is really a demon cloaking itself as a human spirit.

Now there are some Catholics who believe that God may allow a human spirit to return to warn the living about an impending crisis. A ghost that is allowed to do this would be classified in the paranormal world as a messenger ghost and poses no threat to the living.

A malevolent spirit, however, is an entirely different kind of ghost. It is out to do harm and can be often mistaken as a demon by the normal person or improperly trained paranormal investigator.

Herein lies another problem with the Rites of Exorcism: There is no provision in the Rite to get rid of a malevolent spirit, only a demon. It's possible that the Rites of Exorcism will have little to no effect on a once-human malevolent entity. In fact, it could make matters worse in the long run. There are three possible scenarios that could occur if the Rites of Exorcism are used to expel a malevolent spirit. One—the malevolent spirit could leave permanently; two—the Rites of Exorcism will have no effect on the malevolent spirit except maybe to anger it to the point that it ramps up its reign of terror; and three—the Rites of Exorcism may make the malevolent entity leave for a short period of time but come back with a vengeance.

The only good option is that the malevolent entity would leave permanently. Unfortunately, that's the option that's least likely to occur. It's been my experience that even a house blessing by a priest or other member of clergy is enough to anger the malevolent spirit to the point of some type of retaliation.

Now one could argue that the spirit is reacting this way because it's really a demon and not a type of ghost or spirit at all.

Here's the thing: Sometimes a malevolent spirit tries to act like a demon, to make it appear more powerful than it really is. A demon may act as if it is just a ghost or spirit in order to hide how powerful it really is. The objective is the same in both cases: It's an attempt to fool the living. The real trick for the living is being able to tell the difference between a demonic entity and a malevolent spirit.

That is the difference between many well-trained paranormal investigators and a lot of Roman Catholic priests. A properly trained paranormal investigator learns to take their personal belief system out of the equation while working on a case and to deal only with the facts and data they've gathered during the course of an investigation. Many priests, however, will generally only operate within the guidelines of their faith.

There's nothing wrong with having faith and believing in something greater than yourself, but sometimes when dealing with a malevolent spirit or a demon you need not only your faith but the ability to look at all possible scenarios.

Most paranormal investigators, including myself, have bucket-loads of faith, but they also look outside their faith or religion for other explanations in an attempt to do what's best for their client. In other words—not everything that goes bump in the night is a demon—nor is it always a ghost or spirit.

As I write this I can't help but recall a case I worked on many years ago. It concerned two older women who, in their youth, belonged to a group of Satan worshipers. They were now being plagued by what they perceived to be a demonic entity, which would be understandable given their background.

When they first contacted me, they said that they were being physically pushed by something unseen and that objects were being moved or would disappear altogether only to turn up eventually in rather unusual spots. The women were obviously scared.

I set up a time to visit and when my team and I entered the home we couldn't help but notice all the religious items displayed around the house. Bowls of sea salt sat on all the tables and kitchen counters, a bible lay open on the coffee table, crosses and rosaries were everywhere. We found even more bibles and religious items in the bedrooms, bathrooms, dining room, and family room.

The women themselves looked like they'd lived a hard life. Deep wrinkles and creases lined their faces and their hair was white and unkempt. Their eyes were bloodshot and teary—they looked as if they hadn't slept in months.

While the amount and type of paranormal activity the women reported wasn't violent enough or strong enough to even come close to being the work of a demon, we set up our equipment and the team began the investigation.

I took the cup of coffee the women offered and sat down at the kitchen table to find out more about what was happening in their home. They told me about their background and about the one woman's husband who'd died a couple of years ago.

With some prodding, I found out that the deceased husband was an abusive person while he was alive and it became obvious his widow wasn't exactly overcome with grief. It was after the husband's death that her sister moved in with her and the paranormal activity started.

It seemed obvious to me that it wasn't a demon causing all the activity, but the woman's abusive, deceased husband who was responsible. It's been my experience that if someone was a bad person in life, death doesn't do much to change their mood or personality. Try as I might to convince the women that they weren't dealing with a demonic entity but the spirit of the ex-husband, they wouldn't believe me. Left with no other choice, the team and I decided that we'd work within their belief to get rid of the malevolent entity that plagued the property.

I pulled out a ritual I use frequently that will get rid of just about anything. In this case it was going to be like using a sledgehammer to kill a cockroach, but the women had left me no other choice and I was confident it would take care of the malevolent entity in the home.

As I began the ritual, the grandfather clock in the living room struck three; it was one in the afternoon. That gave the team and me pause, but once a ritual is started it's never a good idea to stop, because then it has to be started over.

Further into the ritual one of the team members' telephones went off, indicating a text message. The message was from a friend he hadn't talked to in years and read: "I will be leaving in five minutes." We found out days after the investigation that this friend had never texted the team member that day and hadn't texted or called our team member in months.

Ten minutes later, when I finished the ritual, the house took on an eerie calm, as if time had stopped. Then a shift in energy took place—it was so profound it was palpable.

The energy in the house felt lighter and fresh. Sunshine streamed through the windows, and the heavy, oppressive feeling that had been in the home when we arrived had lifted. The ritual, once again, had worked as it was supposed to. The house was clean.

The women, who also noticed the change in the home's at-mosphere, thanked us profusely for ridding them of the demon and the team packed up and left.

The reason I wanted to tell this story was to illustrate the point that even if something is perceived to be demonic, that isn't always the case. However, perception is reality, and good paranormal investigators operate within their client's reality—not their own.

To me, that is one of the problems with how the Church often handles situations like these. The Church operates within its own belief system and reality and fails, in many cases, to rec-ognize the perception of reality of those it is trying to help.

Exorcism in Different Religions

Different cultures and religions have different ways of dealing with demonic or evil entities. While some may seem brutal, the goal is always the same—get rid of the evil and the chaos that it brings.

Shamanism

This is the earliest recorded method of dealing with evil spirits, or what we would call a demon. In ancient times, it was believed that the evil spirit had a tight grip on a human soul and it was the shaman's job to get rid of it.

The shaman would do this in various ways, depending on their belief system. During the exorcism the demon would at-tempt to communicate with the shaman and perhaps reveal se-crets about the shaman, use physical attacks, or attack the sha-man psychically to make him or her stop the exorcism.

It's believed that the only protection the shamans had at their disposal was their faith and the power of the gifts given to them by whatever higher power they believed in.

Chinese Shamanism

In the native Chinese religious culture, called Taoism, exorcising demons is one of the main focuses. Taoists believe that harmony in the universe must be maintained.

When this harmony is disrupted by an evil entity, the shaman enters a trance to establish a connection between the light and dark, yin and yang, in order to promote the healing process.

Chinese history shows that rituals were performed to summon martial deities from a spiritual group called the Thunder Department, or leibu. These rituals have been used to exorcise the demons that were being blamed for illness, plagues, irregular weather, and other problems in the world.

It was believed that by using the power of thunder the shamans would rely on universally accepted forms of violence to get rid of the demons and return the world to order and harmony.

Korean Shamanism

In the Korean culture, shamanism involves indigenous beliefs, Buddhism, and Taoism. It's believed that the role of the shaman, who is normally a woman, is to act as an intermediary between God, the Gods, and the people.

Korean shamans, or mudangs, may hold services in which illnesses may be cured, local gods are summoned, or sacrifices are made to free someone's ancestors by exorcising evil spirits.

The Korean shamans are similar to the shamans found in Siberia, Manchuria, Mongolia, and such places as the Ryukyu Islands in Japan. The island of Cheju off the coast of South Korea is also a huge center for shamanism—a centuries-old tradition that exists even today.

Native American Shamanism

Most Native American shamans use rituals to purify and cleanse the human body. They focus on using different spiritual methods to treat people who are sick, because it is widely believed that some type of spirit may be the cause of the illness.

In cases where evil or perhaps angry spirits are blamed for the sickness, a special ritual may be performed to exorcise the spirits.

One of the most common rituals involves the use of sage. The sage is burned, because many people believe that burning sage drives any evil spirits from the area to assist in creating a sacred space. This practice is still used today among Native American cultures and people of other spiritual beliefs and is commonly known as smudging.

In some Native American cultures the entire community may be involved in symbolic healing rites in order to exorcise spirits or cure illness.

African Shamanism

It's not unusual for shamans in Africa to also be called witchdoctors, because many people believe the shamans have the power to fight against witchcraft.

In some African tribal cultures, it's believed that demons tend to target children because they are the most vulnerable. In addition, many parts of Africa have a strong belief in witchcraft and witches. Rituals and chants may be utilized by the shaman to drive out the demons, but in some cases violence is resorted to in order to accomplish this task.

For example, peppers could be rubbed into the child's eyes or the child could be threatened with drowning in order to expel the evil spirit residing inside the child.

Shamans may also perform specific rituals to cure illness and other problems the person is experiencing.

Hinduism

The practice of exorcism in Hindu traditions, beliefs, and practices is mainly connected with an ancient culture known as the Dravidians, who lived in the south of India. One of the holy books of the Hindus, the Atharva Veda, is said to hold many secrets pertaining to magic and medicine, and many of those spells are directly related to exorcism and expelling evil spirits.

Vaishnava traditions can use the reciting of the names of Narasimha and the reading of the scriptures of Bhagavata Purana out loud. In addition, the main Vedic book on ghosts and other matters in relation to death, the Garuda Purana, can be used in some cases to rid a person of an evil spirit that has entered their lives or their bodies.

Buddhism

When Buddhism arrived on the scene, it reinforced the use of shamanism. Buddhism stresses the need to achieve moral perfection through reincarnations in order for a human being to reach nirvana. Nirvana is absolute peace and nothingness.

Many Buddhist exorcists work in Japan and the exorcism ritual is performed by a temple's chief priest and their assistant, who read the appropriate scriptures of Buddhism, or sutras, and burn special incense.

The priest may also carry a wooden staff with metal rings attached with thread. When used properly the staff will emit an unearthly sound that is meant to scare away the demons or evil spirits.

Some Buddhist traditions revolving around exorcism may include causing discomfort to the human in order to drive out the demons. This could include fasting, slapping the skin, or putting the person in ice-cold water. All these methods and others are designed to make the demon so uncomfortable it flees the human body it has possessed.

Judaism

In Jewish folklore and the kabbalah, possession is recognized differently than in the Christian sense of the word. It's believed that a living person can become possessed by a spirit called a dybbuk. A dybbuk is the soul of a dead person who returns from Gehanna, or what Christians would call purgatory. This soul who didn't fulfill its purpose during life would attach itself to a living person who is going through something similar to what this spirit was during its life.

This spirit could be good or evil. The good spirit would be a spirit guide to help the living person during their life, while the evil spirit attaches to the living person to cause as much trouble and chaos as possible.

A Jewish exorcism generally involves ten people who gather around the individual who is possessed. The rabbi uses a ram's horn trumpet, referred to as a shofar. The group then says Psalm 91 over and over and the rabbi blows the shofar in a very specific sequence. The blowing of the shofar rattles the possessed person and the spirit who then loosens its grip on the living person. This allows the group to address the living and the dead separately. Psalm 91 deals with abiding in the shadow of the Almighty and can be used as protection against evil. It's also used by some as refuge against the trouble and evils of the world and society.

Once this occurs, the rabbi enters into a conversation with the spirit to determine its purpose and the group begins the healing process, which makes the spirit feel it's accomplished its goal. This same conversation and ritual is performed for the living person as well.

Protestant

There are some Protestant denominations that do recognize possession and exorcism, although it isn't as formal as it is in the Catholic religion. Pentecostal denominations often practice exorcism as a matter of routine during church services, while other Protestant denominations use it sparingly and with an overabundance of caution.

In some Protestant traditions, tests are used to determine if a person is possessed or suffering from a mental or psychological problem or if the problem is spiritual in nature and can be cured by prayer and dousing them with Holy Water. If the alleged possessed person reacts violently to the Holy Water and the name of Jesus, it's assumed the person is possessed by a demonic entity.

Pentecostal

Most Pentecostals believe that Satan is real and that he and his legions of demons spend the majority of their time trying to undermine God and his work.

Unlike some other religions, Pentecostals do not believe that all the suffering in the world is in the minds of humans. Some branches of the Pentecostal religion believe that God does allow some suffering in order to reinforce faith and to assist in building a person's character.

On the other side of the coin are the Pentecostals who believe that God has nothing to do with human suffering but that it is the work of Satan and his demons.

Which side a Pentecostal is on depends on how they interpret certain passages in the bible. One example is 2 Corinthians 12:7–10, which has to do with the thorn in Paul's side. The Pentecostals who believe that God allows for some suffering believe that God himself supplied the thorn, while those who believe suffering is due to demons point out there is nothing in those verses that indicate God supplied the thorn.

Pentecostals generally use the term "deliverance" in place of the word "exorcism." There are certain Pentecostal groups who believe homosexuality is caused by demons and regularly hold gay exorcisms in an effort to help the homosexuals in the Pentecostal religion to get rid of the demon possessing them and causing them to be homosexual.

There are entire Pentecostal denominations in Latin America and Africa devoted to their ability to "cast out demons." This has led to a whole host of problems for those branches of the Pentecostal religion.

There are some Pentecostal churches in Brazil that have their entire congregational activity focused around Satan and other evil spirits during a specified day. Not unlike in other religions, only church-approved pastors are allowed to perform these rituals.

In some Pentecostal churches the congregation uses rose petals, Holy Water, sanctified oil, bread, and tree branches to perform the deliverance.

Roman Catholic

This is the type of exorcism most common on television and in the movies. In the Catholic Church, exorcisms can only be performed by an ordained priest or a higher prelate with permission of the local bishop. In the majority of cases the bishop will only give his consent once all other avenues have been exhausted, such as extensive medical tests to ensure the person is not suffering from a mental illness.

In the Roman Catholicritual, specific symptoms of possession are listed as being possible signs of demonic possession. These include speaking a foreign or ancient language that the possessed person has no knowledge of, extraordinary strength, aversion to anything holy, profuse blasphemy, and sacrilege. Keep in mind this list is not all-inclusive.

Normally the Catholic Church uses a document called "Of Exorcisms and Certain Supplications" that contains specific prayers, blessings, and invocations that are meant to expel the demon from the possessed place or person.

While Lucifer, or Satan, as he is sometimes called, doesn't appear often or isn't referred to by name many times in the Holy Bible, it's apparent that his presence is there, being told through the stories and experiences the people are having.

I read once that sometime in the early history of the Catholic Church it had named about twenty thousand demons and believed they had just scratched the surface. Now isn't that just a real scary thought?

STORIES OF EXORCISMS

Documents tell us that exorcisms have been used throughout history as a cure for many things. Most of these exorcisms occurred before modern society's advancements in medicine and psychology. It's difficult to imagine that in some cases, exorcisms are still used today because it's believed that a demon is causing certain conditions. Here's a brief look at just such cases.

Innocent Life Lost

In 2003 at a church in the Midwest, a young boy, eight years old, was suffering from autism. He was accidently killed when church members bound the boy tightly in sheets and held him down because they believed that a demon or another type of malevolent spirit was responsible for the child's autism and that an exorcism could cure him of his ailment.

The autopsy showed extensive bruising on the back of the boy's neck and the official cause of death was listed as asphyxiation.

There is nothing wrong with having strong religious beliefs, but there comes a time when you have to use common sense and realize that sometimes the methods used in some of these churches, no matter what their intentions, are not the best course of action for the person they profess they want to help.

I can't even begin imagine the terror that poor child experienced in the last moments of his short life.

A Case of Deliverance?

As stated in the previous chapter, there are some in the Pentecostal religion who believe that a rite of deliverance can exorcise the demons that can cause someone to be a homosexual. The amazing part is that many Pentecostal homosexuals are subjecting themselves to this ritual. This is one such story.

Matthew, a devout Pentecostal, was excited to get to church to see a prophet who was visiting from out of state. He'd been having trouble focusing at work and in his personal life, so the thought of getting some insight from the prophet appealed to him.

When the time came, he got in line behind some of the other parishioners for his chance to talk to this powerful prophet. As he approached, the prophet asked him if he was gay, to which he responded in the affirmative.

The prophet declared that he needed to undergo a deliverance to rid him of his homosexual ways and all would become clear to him. According to the Pentecostal church dogma, being a homosexual is a sin put upon some humans by demons who possess them and make them act against God's word. Many Pentecostals view the act of deliverance as one of love and caring, meant to save the person from the influence of demons.

While Matthew was a little hesitant, he began to think that something was wrong with him and maybe this prophet could deliver him from the demon that could have been tormenting him most of his life.

This would be at least the tenth time he'd undergone a gay exorcism since he'd turned about sixteen, but Matthew thought that maybe this powerful prophet could finally deliver him from his homosexuality. Just as before, the deliverance didn't have the desired effect.

When all of this had started a few years previously, Matthew wasn't convinced that one could be delivered from being gay. However, he'd been raped at one point in his short life, and thought that maybe that had something to do with his homosexuality, even though he'd felt an attraction to other boys long before the rape occurred.

However, as Matthew grew older he began to have doubts and became frightened that maybe he could be possessed. That's when all of the exorcisms started.

The exorcisms continued off and on for a couple of years. The last time the prophet tried to exorcise Matthew was at her house. She put oil on his head and began praying, pressing on his head and stomach.

Matthew fled to the bathroom and began vomiting as the prophet continued the exorcism. At one point he believed something inside him began to scream—a guttural, organic scream that seemed to rise from somewhere deep inside.

Sometime during the exorcism, the prophet asked for the name of the demon and claimed the demon revealed his name in Latin. To this day the prophet won't reveal what the demon said.

As all the successive exorcisms failed, Matthew became extremely depressed. His mother forced him to stop seeing his boyfriend, and one day at school he had a nervous breakdown. He was then put into a hospital for a few months to recover and regain all the weight he'd lost during his depression.

After that Matthew began dressing in drag and even showed up in church wearing makeup, a wig, and women's clothes. The elders of the church wouldn't let him even enter the building.

Matthew's family urged him to get another exorcism and he refused. After that, his father kicked him out of the house and he spent a night in a homeless shelter before entering a psychiatric hospital at the urging of a counselor.

During his stay in the hospital, Matthew came to terms with his homosexuality and went on to live by himself in a meagerly furnished apartment while he attended college.

While he still attends church with his family, he refuses all attempts by the church to have him undergo another exorcism. Matthew is finally at peace with who he is.

As for the prophet, she now believes that Matthew didn't want to be delivered, and thinks that a deliverance will only work if the person truly wants to be delivered from the demons that plague their lives.

Unfortunately or fortunately, depending on your point of view, Matthew is not the only person who has undergone multiple deliverances in certain Pentecostal churches. Each year, hundreds of gay men line up at special "gay deliverance" nights in hopes of driving out the demon that they may believe is causing their homosexuality.

I think what bothers me the most is that, judging from this story, a lot of men don't start to seek out a gay deliverance until their church or some other entity or person makes them doubt themselves and wonder if something is wrong with them, such as being possessed by a demon that may be causing their homo-sexuality.

Exorcisms that Kill

Throughout the years, well-meaning but misguided people have tried to exorcise demons out of people who were believed to be possessed or suffering from some other perceived ailment or malady. However, in many cases, these people have ended up killing the person they were trying to save. Here are some short stories of exorcisms that resulted in death.

Witchcraft Be Gone

An interesting case out of England tells of two immigrants from the Congo who were convinced one of their brothers, a fifteen-year-old, was guilty of bringing witchcraft into their home.

The female siblings used knives, sticks, metal bars, and a hammer and chisel to torture their brother. Their brother begged for death before drowning in the bathtub. Apparently the older siblings believed that their actions would cause an exorcism to occur and make their brother stop his evil ways.

Now, as strange as this may sound to Western culture, a poll conducted in 2010 found that over half of people living in sub-Saharan Africa believe in witchcraft. However, I was a bit confused about why the girls thought an exorcism would stop their brother from practicing witchcraft. Perhaps they believed that the only reason their brother would bring witchcraft into the home was if he was possessed.

A Crucifixion?

As recently as 2005, in a small convent in Europe, a young woman claimed she was hearing Satan telling her that she was acting in a sinful manner.

In an attempt to help this woman, a number of nuns and a priest tied the girl to a cross, stuffed a towel in her mouth, and left her alone for three days without food or water. The nuns and priest believed this was the best way to drive the demons out of this poor young woman.

However, the woman, who had a long history of being schizophrenic, died from dehydration and suffocation.

When I first heard about this story I had to double check the date, because to me it sounded like something that would have happened in days long ago and not in modern society. It almost sounds like a form of crucifixion, not an exorcism. In addition, I find it hard to believe that many churches would condone or sanction such actions by one of their priests and/or nuns.

Short News Articles
about Exorcisms that Caused a Death

In October of 1997, the *Los Angeles Times* contained a story about a five-year-old girl named Marie who was literally beaten to death by her mother and two of the mother's friends. The trio, who'd been doing methamphetamine, was "beating the devil" out of the girl at the time the death occurred. According to the story, the two friends encouraged the mother to beat the girl harder while the mother repeatedly beat the child's bottom with a wooden paddle. In addition, the trio jumped on the young child's back. A trial was held and the trio was convicted of murder.

In September of 1998, the *Scotsman* published a sad story about the death of a five-year-old boy in South London. The boy's mother, a Nigerian immigrant, choked her "naughty" boy to death because she believed it would force the demons out of his tiny body. Believing that the boy would be healed, she kept his lifeless body in her apartment for a few days. The mother was sent to a psychiatric unit.

The *Japan Times* reported a story about six decomposing bodies found at the home of a faith healer in July 1995. Upon the conclusion of a police investigation, the healer and three of her followers were arrested. When interrogated, the healer told police that she would beat her followers to exorcise the evil spirits that resided in their bodies. The faith healer received the death sentence, while her followers received prison sentences.

In April of 1996, the *United Press International* (UPI) picked up a story about the death of a thirty-eight-year-old mother of two in Thailand. She died because her family suggested that she seek out the help of a shaman because she had occasional hysterical outbursts. The shaman told the family that the woman was possessed by an evil spirit that devoured human intestines. The shaman beat her about the face and genitals with a dried stingray tail. The woman escaped after two days of beatings, and the family refused to pay for the exorcism. Because they failed to pay, the shaman abducted the woman and continued with more brutal, ritualistic beatings until the woman died. The police charged the shaman with murder.

In September of 1994, the *Guardian* ran a story about a woman who believed her body had been taken over by worms and snakes. Thinking that she'd been taken over by evil spirits, she sought the help of her brother, who believed that at one time he'd been possessed. The brother's neighbors heard horrible screams coming from the brother's house and saw him stomping on something. Needless to say the woman died from injuries that included multiple fractured ribs, massive internal injuries, and a lacerated liver. The brother claimed that he'd been attempting to stomp out the evil spirits that took over his sister. He ended up spending a mere five years in jail for the death of his sister.

In January and March of 1996, the *Agence France-Presse* (AFP) relayed the story of a Muslim fundamentalist group in Egypt that had four of its members sentenced to ten years of hard labor in prison for murdering a ten-year-old girl they were attempting to exorcise. Certain faith healers in Egypt ended up killing forty-seven people and injuring another ninety-eight in 1995 by beating them to get rid of the evil spirits they believed were inhabiting the people's bodies. Included in the injured people were eleven who'd gone blind. In just 1995 alone, the police arrested a total of 224 faith healers.

In September of 1994, the AFP in Cairo reported a story of two daughters punching their mother to death because they believed she was possessed by a djinn, which is a type of genie. They said their mother often said things that made no sense and they "decided to expel the djinn from their mother so she would return to her normal state." Both girls were sent to a mental hospital.

In July of 1996, the *LA Times* ran a story about a South Korean immigrant who died in California from extensive internal injuries. She suffered those fatal injuries while her husband, a deacon from her church, and a Korean missionary attempted to perform an exorcism on the woman in a two-day ritual. The men used their hands and feet to try to rid the woman of evil spirits. She participated in one of the three-hour sessions, but didn't want to do the two other three-hour-long sessions. During the postmortem examination it was found that she had sixteen broken ribs and her lungs had collapsed. The court found two of the three men guilty of manslaughter.

In May of 1997, the *Victoria (BC) Times-Colonist* and *Toronto Globe & Mail* both reported the death of a forty-five-year-old man on the Sheguiandah reserve on Manitoulin Island, Ontario. The story tells of a nineteen-year-old man who believed the elder man was a bearwalker. In their culture, a bearwalker is a powerful demon who is able to shape-shift and uses a form of sorcery to make people sick and even kill them. The judge in the case acquitted the young man, who beat the elder to death with a bat-sized whale bone. The judge ruled that the young man truly believed that he was in mortal danger and was defending himself.

In December of 1998, the *Daily Telepgraph* printed a news story about the deaths of three adults and three children by the United Pentecostal of Brazil, which had a congregation of thirty people. All six people were killed by a pastor and his followers at a remote rubber plantation. The pastor believed he heard voices from Jesus telling him that the former pastor and his followers be punished. The people were beaten to death through whipping and stamping; the killers believed they were ridding these people of evil spirits that possessed them. After the initial beatings, some of the people were moved to nearby shacks and tortured until they died. The deaths were only confirmed by the police after one man escaped with the details of the killings.

In both October and December of 1995, the *Guardian* told the story of a twenty-seven-year-old man named Nick who lived in East London. Nick believed his fiancée was possessed by Satan after she refused to marry him. Nick was a renegade Baptist and got one of his disciples to help him perform an exorcism on his fiancée. According to the disciple, Nick locked his fiancée in his bedroom for fourteen days, where he starved and beat her repeatedly. In addition, he force-fed her "communion" wine and bread. The disciple reported that after Nick said, "In the name of Jesus Christ, I command the Angels of Execution to kill this body," the young woman died. The disciple reported that they tried to resurrect her for three days. When that wasn't successful, they sealed her body in a back room of a house that Nick had converted into his church. Nick was sentenced to six years in jail, while his disciple only served eighteen months.

In March of 1999, *El Pais*, a Spanish newspaper, reported on the death of a Belgian woman who died in Spain. She was suffocated during an apparent sect ritual that was meant to "purify" her body. It's believed that the woman was the victim of a ceremony practiced by this sect that involves wrapping someone in a blanket and then sitting on them. This, obviously, would interrupt her breathing and cause an oxygen shortage that eventually would cause the body to convulse and then result in urination and defecation. This sect believes that this "purification" can cause a person to live longer. In this victim's case, however, she went into cardiac arrest. The three who participated in the ritual, including the woman's husband, were detained by police. The victim's mother stated that her daughter didn't belong to a sect.

In 1995, *Knight-Ridder Newspapers* told the story of the death of a young Korean woman living in California. The twenty-five-year-old had suffered for years with insomnia, and medications were ineffective. Her family took her to see a minister of a fifteen-member sect called Jesus-Amen Ministries. The minister said that the young woman was possessed by demons and would have to undergo an exorcism. The woman's mother and three other women beat the woman on the chest and face at least one hundred times, breaking over ten ribs. The young woman finally died. Some members of the sect stayed with the young woman's body for five days because the minister said the woman's spirit had gone on a "heavenly journey" and they should wait for it to come back.

In 1997, the *New York Daily News* carried a story about the tragic death of a five-year-old girl when the child's mother and grandmother attempted to exorcise the "demons out of her" that they believed caused her to have tantrums. The two women tied the girl down and forced her to ingest a lethal mixture of ammonia, vinegar, cayenne pepper, black pepper, and olive oil. They went as far as to tape the child's mouth shut so she couldn't spit out the potion. After the five-year-old died, the mother and grandmother panicked and wrapped her body in plastic and left it out for trash pickup. The police who investigated the matter charged both women with second-degree murder and depraved indifference.

In July of 1994, the AFP picked up a story about a woman of Algerian descent who died in northern France. According to the article, the woman suffered from a form of epileptic seizures since undergoing brain surgery in 1993. Her brother, convinced his sister was possessed by a demon, called in an exorcist—the head of a local mosque. The alleged exorcist tortured the young woman for hours. They made her drink gallons of salt water, beat the bottoms of her feet, and squeezed her in the neck region, all in an attempt to exorcise the demon. The exorcist, his assistant, and the brother were all charged with murder.

Between October of 1995 and January of 1996, newspapers such as the *Daily Telegraph*, *Daily Mail*, *Scotsman*, *Independent*, and the *Guardian* ran news stories about a woman from East London who believed she was possessed by djinns. She claimed the djinns threatened to cut out her tongue if she said praises to Allah. She'd been married the year before in India, but immigration problems prevented her husband from joining her in England. The family claimed that the woman's face would become distorted, she would talk in a man's voice, have the posture of an old woman, and talked repeatedly about djinns pushing her. In desperation, the family called in a Syrian woman who was a Sunni Muslim. The exorcist said the woman needed an exorcism and with the help of her friend and the victim's sister and brother, the exorcism began. The victim was repeatedly beaten with a plastic vacuum cleaner pipe and cane for over five hours with readings from the Koran. The attack continued for a period of about four hours the following day. One of the participants in the exorcism also jumped up and down on the victim's stomach and chest, fracturing multiple ribs. The victim died. All three of the participants were found guilty of manslaughter. The Syrian woman was sentenced to seven years, the victim's sister to three years, and her brother to one year in prison.

In November of 1994, a sad but interesting story came out of New Zealand. According to the article, Jan and Pete Wilson joined a fundamentalist Apostolic Church in 1993. Jan, believing the church had cured her bad back during a few faith healing sessions, began to attend the church on a regular basis. By early 1994, the Wilsons were completely entrenched in the church. One day in May, Pete stayed home because his wife told him that if he went to work the demons would get him.

The problem was that by this time, Jan was completely convinced that she was God, and she'd convinced Pete of that fact as well and he had gone so far as to call her God instead of Jan.

Jan, convinced her two-year-old was filled with the devil, slapped the toddler across the face for about ten minutes in an effort to rid her of demons. Jan commanded that her seventeen-year-old daughter hold the two-year-old down while she administered the slapping. Finally the older daughter left the house in tears.

Later that same day, Jason, who worked with Pete, stopped by the house to see if he was okay. As soon as Jason entered the house, Jan commanded that he kneel before her and yelled, "I can feel Jesus in the tips of these fingers!" Just then Pete appeared from the other room and was chanting. Pete raised Jason's shirt and squeezed his stomach, ordering him to vomit because he was possessed. While this was going on, Jan slapped Jason's face.

Jason fled the mad scene and reported the events to his boss, who ran over to Pete's house only to find him vomiting in a bucket. All the time Jan was screaming at Pete, "This is what happens when you sin!"

Alarmed, Pete's boss left the house and immediately called the police, and that evening a social worker, a doctor, a mental health professional, and three police officers visited the house. When they arrived, Jan told one of the police officers that he was possessed. The mental health person pleaded with the doctor to issue a certificate that would allow Jan to be detained, but the doctor refused, saying that Jan was just a religious fanatic. The police found a number of firearms in the house and removed them before leaving.

The next morning Jan and Pete were totally convinced they were completely surrounded by demons, so they smashed their dishes, burned the furniture, and threw their belongings out of the house. They also made their children participate in this activity.

In addition, Pete took the kids' pet mice outside, claiming they were evil, and tore their heads and tails off and then buried the bodies in two different holes in the yard. The family ate, but Jan ordered them to vomit up the food and "piss their pants." Jan then took all the clothes off her son and threw him outside in the cold and darkness. He found a piece of clothing that had been thrown out of the house earlier and put it on.

Jan then said that her son was the devil incarnate and forced Pete to hold their son down so she could perform an exorcism. Pete held him down so strongly that the child's wrist was broken. Jan grabbed a concrete block and struck her son in the head with it several times. The little boy was screaming and begging for help and saying that he believed.

Scared by the horrible screams, the neighbors called the police. When the police arrived they found Pete, naked and holding down his son, who by this time was barely clinging to life. Pete refused to look up at his wife because he felt it would be blasphemy to look at "God." When the ambulance finally arrived Jan screamed at them, "He's already dead. We killed him, you stupid man, like the first Jesus."

STORIES OF EXORCISMS 151

In November, Pete and Jan were found not guilty of murder; the judge claimed they were victims of a folie à deux, which is defined as madness shared by two.

Exorcisms Gone Bad

The world is filled with stories of exorcisms from all different cultures and religions. Like with almost everything else, there is no guarantee that an exorcism will work one hundred percent of the time. Sometimes, unlike what is always depicted on television, movies, and other media outlets, exorcisms go wrong—extremely wrong. These cases are meant to illustrate the extremes some people will take to rid someone of what they perceive to be a demonic entity. Let's take a look at a few such cases.

Cell Phone Hell

I found a news article recently that told of a priest in Europe who was receiving text messages from a young woman possessed by a demon.

It appears that this priest tried to exorcise a demon from this woman and the exorcism was unsuccessful. As a result, the demon was influencing the girl into sending hateful and threatening text messages to the priest.

One of the texts allegedly read, "She will not come out of this hell. She's mine. Anyone who prays for her will die."

After the priest texted the number back, another message is supposed to have said, "Shut up, preacher. You cannot save yourself. Idiot. You pathetic old preacher."

The priest had not given any specifics as to how he was going to try to help this poor woman, but he was convinced she needed additional help and was completely possessed. It was also believed that the girl might not have even been aware her cell phone was being used in this manner or for this purpose.

The article didn't state whether or not this priest was going to attempt another exorcism.

Although sparse on details, this case does present some interesting questions and possibilities. As with any exorcism, whoever performs it always expects some type of backlash or retaliation. It would appear that if indeed this girl was possessed, that the demon was threatening to possess the priest and maybe even kill him.

While these types of threats may not be unusual in such a situation, the method in which the threats are being delivered is unusual.

To me the question becomes: Is the demon using its victim to send the messages to the priest via cell phone, or, in the alternative, is the girl not possessed at all, but sending the text messages herself?

It's also possible that the girl isn't possessed but is being repressed or otherwise influenced by the demonic entity to send the text messages.

The answers to these questions may never be known, at least by us. However, it is still an interesting case in an exorcism gone wrong.

Family Flees from House

In the British Isles, a family has taken up residence in a rented home because their home is too haunted for them to stay. Here's the story:

For over twenty years Mark and Darcy lived in their home peacefully and without incident. But one day everything changed.

Darcy was taking a break from doing her daily cleaning and sat down at the table to rest. She was quickly overcome by a strange feeling, and she felt as if her chair was shaking. The tablecloth fell to the floor as if it'd been pulled. It was then that Darcy claimed the room went out of focus.

Fighting to get it together, Darcy then saw a mist come through the kitchen window and slowly form into three ghosts. She claimed they were the ghost of a man in his late twenties/early thirties, a woman about the same age, and a little girl of about six. Absolutely scared out of her wits, Darcy screamed and ran from her home.

When Mark came home, Darcy was still shaking in fear and quite hysterical. It took Mark a considerable amount of time to get her calmed down enough to tell him what happened.

Mark, not believing they had ghosts, suggested that Darcy see a doctor, which she did. The doctor prescribed an antidepressant for her. However, there aren't any pills in the world that are going to cure a haunted house, and the ghostly activity not only continued, it increased.

Scraping noises and eerie balls of light would occur almost constantly when Darcy was alone. She also experienced the sensation of someone breathing heavily in her face, pulling at her clothing, and the male ghost pinning her down on the couch.

If that wasn't enough, the male ghost began to put his hand on Darcy's thigh and make other sexual advances.

Darcy noticed that Mark's behavior began to change as well. Once a sweet, gentle man, Mark was becoming aggressive and prone to losing his temper over every little thing—this behavior was definitely out of his normal character and Darcy became so concerned she called in a Catholic priest to get the ghosts out of her house through an exorcism. Armed with a bible and gallons of Holy Water, the priest went to the house.

After the priest visited, things calmed down for a short period of time but began again in earnest, which caused Darcy to convince Mark to leave the house; they haven't returned in well over a year.

Now, not having been at the location or speaking personally to Mark and Darcy, I can only speak to the facts as they were presented in the news article I read—but those facts speak volumes.

First, I'm a bit unsure as to whether the priest did an exorcism or simply did a house blessing. I just can't imagine the Church authorizing an exorcism when there are no apparent signs of demonic activity—simply ghostly activity. I would be more inclined to say the priest simply blessed the house, which could cause the paranormal activity in the home to subside for a period of time. However, with a persistent-enough ghost, which this one obviously was, the activity may not only come back but return with a vengeance and actually be worse than it was before.

In addition, an exorcism doesn't appear to work on ghosts as well as it works on demons; it wasn't designed to. While the Rite of Exorcism is extremely powerful, it may have little effect on a ghost. There are other rituals that can be performed to get rid of a malevolent spirit; however, those rituals aren't generally performed by the Roman Catholic Church.

What I find the most curious is the apparent change in Mark's behavior from a teddy bear of a guy into a bear of a man. These behavioral changes could be attributed to a few things. It could just be the stress of living in an extremely haunted house.

If the activity was occurring at all times of the day and night, sleep deprivation could be a logical explanation for the sudden changes in Mark's demeanor.

The male spirit in the home could have been influencing Mark in some way, causing him to act in a way that wasn't normal for his character. There have been other cases where this has happened, so it's not out of the realm of possibility. Coming under the influence of a spirit is a lot easier than many people realize, but it's important to remember that being influenced by a ghost or spirit doesn't mean the spirit is attached to that person.

The last possibility is spirit attachment. It's possible that the ghost of the man could have attached himself to Mark, causing the changes in behavior, but in this case I just don't believe that's what happened, and this is why: In the case of a spirit attachment, just because you physically move from one location to another, normally the spirit attachment will continue because the spirit is attached to a person, not a particular location. Because there haven't been any reported incidents since Mark and Darcy left their home, a case of spirit attachment would be unlikely.

Do-It-Yourself Exorcism Gone Wrong

A family on the East Coast told police that their father performed an exorcism on his son, who he felt was possessed because his mother was acting strangely. However, the demon had left their brother and jumped into their mother.

The woman's husband was the only one who could see the demon and was burning leaves and screaming at the demon. In an act of desperation, he rammed two steel crosses down his wife's throat, puncturing her esophagus.

The police found the woman on the front porch bleeding profusely from the mouth. The woman was rushed to the hospital in critical condition, and survived. This exorcism was witnessed by the woman's father-in-law, brother-in-law, and a number of children under the age of ten.

Demonic Possession, Multiple Personality Disorder, or Schizophrenia?

A man involved with a small religious sect returned home one day to find his wife, Maria, who'd been diagnosed with schizophrenia a few years before, barefoot in a farmer's field, doing a strange dance and making bizarre noises.

This man, Floyd, immediately called a member of his church, Rodger, who rushed to the house. Upon observing Maria, Rodger diagnosed Maria as being demonically possessed.

For three days the two men and Rodger's wife read the bible, sang hymns, and ordered the demons to leave Maria. When it was apparent that this wasn't working, two more members of the church were called in to assist.

They tied Maria to a mattress that faced east-west because they believed that by pointing the mattress in that direction Maria couldn't gather strength from any evil spirits, which they believed came out of the north.

Over a short period of time her stomach swelled, and she displayed superhuman strength and talked in strange voices. Floyd claimed that she was possessed by at least eight or ten demons.

Floyd also claimed that Maria was possessed by two princesses who Rodger said had attached themselves to Maria's womb when she was only three and ever since had been fighting to control her.

After a few days with no success, the group called in two amateur exorcists, Bob and Jim. Even though it was their first exorcism, they immediately took control of the situation and ordered that all of Maria's possessions, even her plants, be destroyed.

For over two hours they shouted at the demon to depart and all left Maria except for the two princesses, who Jim claimed were in her womb clinging to each other desperately.

All observers present held Maria down on the bed and pressed hard on her stomach area in an attempt to force the two princesses out of her body. They forced her mouth and eyes to remain open.

Maria cried and hissed and the observers took this behavior as a sign that the demons were being forced out of her body. However, that wasn't the case, and a day later Maria made a final guttural sound and died.

Bob told Floyd not to be distressed because God would bring Maria back to life in a very short period of time, but that never happened and two days later the group reported the death to the authorities.

Floyd and Rodger were found guilty of unlawful imprisonment, while Bob and Jim were convicted of manslaughter.

Exorcisms that Worked

The Terrifying Case of Amelia Summers

In the late 1920s, an exorcism took place at a now nonexistent convent in the Northwest that lasted twenty-three days, unusually long for an exorcism. After all these years the truth about what really happened during that period of time could be hard to ascertain; however, Papal records do state that the Church-sanctioned exorcism occurred. All we have to go on is a small booklet from a witness to the exorcism of Amelia Summers.

The story goes that Amelia was possessed most of her life due to the fact that her aunt was allegedly a witch and put a spell on some herbs that she then placed in Amelia's food. A Capuchin priest was called in and performed an exorcism in 1912, which was successful.

Amelia became possessed again because of curses put on her by her father. While the nature of the curses and reasons for them are unclear, evidently they were effective. The exorcism, which is the focus of this story, took place in three stages sometime between August 18 and December 22.

The small booklet that talks about the case of Amelia states that she was a God-fearing woman who wanted to go to church; however, she felt as if something was holding her back and preventing her from worshipping the Lord.

Amelia also began to hear some inner voice that suggested that she do some rather unspeakable things and she became almost frantic and felt helpless to do anything about what was happening to her. Eventually she began to feel as if she was going insane.

There were many times that Amelia felt the urge to break the container holding her Holy Water and attack her reverend, and she even heard suggestions that she should tear down the church. By the time the priest got to Amelia she hadn't gotten a good night's sleep in almost twenty-six years due to the relentless voices inside her head.

What convinced the priest to request permission from the Church to perform the exorcism was that Amelia displayed many of the classic signs of possession: She would swear whenever religious items were brought near her; she could detect food that had been blessed and refused to eat it; she foamed at the mouth and made a variety of animalistic sounds. Amelia had also become capable of understanding and speaking Latin and other ancient languages that she'd had no prior knowledge of, and on more than one occasion she was levitated to the ceiling in front of several witnesses.

During the exorcism itself, the nuns busied themselves emptying buckets full of horrible-smelling green vomit that Amelia was throwing up, even though she hadn't eaten any food for days.

Amelia's body was so swollen that the people present at the exorcism were afraid she would burst open. Witnesses experienced loud noises, extremely foul smells, and suffered verbal abuse from the demon inside Amelia in the form of threats of death. They also noticed a small lump that seemed to move around her body with no rhyme or reason.

Witnesses also noted that several times the demons would appear to leave Amelia's body; however, this behavior was only an attempt to fool the exorcist into believing his job was done.

With one final prayer the priest forced the demons out of Amelia. This was accompanied by a piercing scream, and voices of the demons yelling in protest. Finally she collapsed on the bed, free of the demons that had possessed her body for most of her life.

For the rest of her life Amelia was able to attend church and partake in other holy rituals.

Obviously, in this case this poor girl was clearly possessed by one or more demonic entities. The question in this case is how Amelia became possessed in the first place.

While it's somewhat unlikely that witchcraft and curses caused the demons to be lured to the house, it's not out of the realm of possibility. Using the facts as they were presented to me, I'd be more inclined to believe that the demons were drawn to Amelia's house, because it's pretty obvious that her family was not only highly dysfunctional, but probably abusive.

This type of negative activity and the emotions that go along with it would have been more than enough to entice the demon to take up residence and possess the most vulnerable person living in the home, and the obvious target of parental and family abuse—Amelia.

South African Exorcism

Back around the turn of the century, in the early 1900s, a young girl named Sara went into a confessional and told the priest that she'd made a pact with the devil. Little is known about Sara other than she was orphaned as a baby and began attending a Mission school at the tender age of four. At the time of the confessional, Sara was sixteen years old.

The Father, not thinking too much about Sara's confession, went on about his business. It wasn't long after that when the nuns at the school began to notice Sara's behavior was becoming erratic and she was acting out of character. Sara was ripping at her clothes, making animal noises, and having conversations with beings that no one else could see. At one point, Sara begged the nuns to call the Father because she claimed, "Quick, quick, or Satan will kill me. He has me in his power! Nothing is blessed with me; I have thrown away all the medals you gave me." She was later heard to exclaim, "You have betrayed me. You promised me days of glory, but now you treat me cruelly."

The Father and nuns became so concerned with Sara's behavior that they felt she might have gone insane.

In the days and weeks to follow, Sara's bizarre behavior increased to alarming levels. The nuns said that Sara's skin would appear to burn if she was sprinkled with Holy Water and she would have a violent reaction when in the presence of crosses or other religious objects, even if the religious items were concealed.

It wasn't long before Sara developed the ability to speak several languages that she'd had no prior knowledge of. She also developed clairvoyance and could relate private details of people's lives that she would have no way of knowing.

In addition, on several occasions Sara exhibited superhuman strength and could easily overpower the adults who tried to restrain her. There were also reports that on several occasions witnesses saw her levitate several feet into the air and would come down when Holy Water was thrown at her.

It didn't take long for the Father to come to the conclusion that Sara was possessed, and he and another priest got permission to perform the Rites of Exorcism in an attempt to save her.

The exorcism took place in two separate sessions on September 11. During the exorcism, Sara knocked a bible out of one of the priest's hands and tried to strangle him with his sacred stole.

The next morning, the priests once again tried to exorcise the demon who appeared to have Sara in his control. This time the demon told the priests that he would signal his departure by performing an act of levitation.

The demon held true to his word by levitating Sara in front of over one hundred witnesses before departing her body.

As a side note, less than a year later Sara allegedly made another pact with the devil and another two-day exorcism followed. Once again the demon departed amid a horrific odor. There is no other information as to the final fate of Sara, although no further incidents of paranormal activity around Sara were recorded.

An American Exorcism

At a prominent medical college in the 1980s, a woman was studied by a group of priests, nuns, psychiatrists, and deacons for signs of demonic possession.

How she became possessed is almost as interesting as the possession itself. This woman, whom I'll call Kathy, had a long history of being involved with various Satanic groups over the previous few years. Apparently the old adage is true: When you play with fire, you're going to get burned.

From the beginning of her counseling with the Roman Catholic Church, Kathy maintained that she was the victim of a demonic attack and requested an exorcism.

Doing their due diligence, the Church wanted to ensure that Kathy wasn't delusional, suffering from a mental illness, or simply seeking attention. Thus she ended up under observation by the group of people mentioned at the beginning of this story.

Those concerned claim that frequently Kathy would go into a trance-like state and not have any memory of anything she said or did during that time. Sometimes while in the trance, Kathy, in a voice that was sometimes higher or lower than her own natural voice, and frequently accompanied by guttural sounds, would tell the observers to "Leave her alone, you idiot." "She's ours." "Leave, you imbecile priest." Or just, "Leave."

At other times during this trance state Kathy would relay personal information about the observers and their families that she had no way of knowing. At other times she would speak in a foreign language.

On one occasion, Kathy displayed knowledge about one of the observer's two cats, which had mysteriously attacked each other in the early morning hours of that day.

Kathy would also levitate off the floor or bed and objects would fly off shelves, seemingly by themselves. During these trance states, she would react negatively to any religious items that were brought into the room; this behavior was often accompanied by verbal threats and/or blasphemous comments hurled at the observers.

Once it was determined by all involved that Kathy was indeed suffering from demonic possession, the priests and nuns prepared themselves to perform the Rites of Exorcism.

The exorcism itself began on a warm summer day, and even though the weather was delightful, once the exorcism began, the participants noticed that the room became increasingly cold, almost to the point of frigid.

Kathy slipped into a quiet trance-like state and while the Rites were being read she began to talk in multiple voices and make unearthly sounds. As this continued the room went from terrible cold to sweltering heat.

Soon the nuns, priests, and others holding Kathy down to prevent her from hurting herself and others began to have a hard time controlling the woman because she'd developed almost superhuman strength. She also began talking in Latin and Spanish—two languages that Kathy had no prior history of speaking.

As far as anyone knows, Kathy has recovered from her ordeal and has returned to a normal life—hopefully free of any involvement in Satanic groups or rituals.

While it's rather obvious that Kathy was suffering from demonic possession, what I find the most fascinating about this case is that it took place at a medical college under the observation of at least one psychiatrist.

It's very rare for the worlds of psychiatry and demonology to collide and then come together to help a poor woman suffering from demonic possession.

One can only hope that this case is not the last one that we'll see when the medical profession, the world of the paranormal, and the Church all work together toward a common goal.

The Curious Case of Frank Lucas

In the late 18th century, the neighbors of Frank Lucas noticed he began to act strangely. He would sing in a different voice, speak a language he normally wouldn't know, and claim to be possessed.

His neighbors contacted the Church and asked them to help Frank, who was a shoemaker by trade. Instead of stepping in to perform an exorcism, the Church sent him to a mental health hospital. Frank spent almost two years at the mental health facility before he was released. The doctors there claimed they could do nothing for poor Frank, and they were convinced that he was possessed by a demon.

During his hospital stay, Frank would become very violent and claim that he was Satan himself. He'd also bark like a dog and sing church hymns backwards. He also claimed that he was possessed by six demons and it would take exactly six priests to get them out of his body.

The Church finally intervened and six priests performed six exorcisms. When the Rite was over, Frank declared that he was free from the demons and thanked the priests profusely before blessing God and running out of the church.

It is believed that Frank was cured of his possession, as he doesn't appear in Church records as ever being possessed again.

The Interesting Case of Mary Parks

Mary was born into a dysfunctional middle-class family in the Midwest and had a troublesome childhood. Her father, a non-practicing Catholic, and her mother, a Southern Lutheran, had Mary baptized in the Lutheran church.

When Mary became a teenager, the family began to experience strange activity in their home. They would hear scratching sounds in the attic and walls. Believing they had a pest problem, they contacted an exterminator.

The pest control company could find no sign of rodents, bats, or any other creature in the home that could be causing the noises. A few days after the exterminator left, the problems became worse. They would hear footsteps in the rooms and hallways, and objects and furniture would move on their own. At times, Mary's bed was shaken so violently she was unable to sleep. Her covers were pulled off of her at night and no matter how tightly she hung onto them, the intensity would increase to a point that she was flung to the floor on several occasions.

At first Mary's parents attributed the activity to her uncle, who'd passed away a few weeks before all the activity started. Mary's Uncle Rex had been a spiritualist and the girl had spent hours with him talking about the paranormal and using a Ouija board to communicate with spirits. Mary had been fascinated by her Uncle Rex and his teachings.

After a few months, however, Mary's parents realized that they were dealing with something far more sinister than Uncle Rex; they believed they were dealing with some type of evil entity, so they sought the help of a Lutheran minister.

The minister prayed with the family in their home and then with just Mary present. They prayed in the church and with the congregation, but the torment of Mary at all hours of the day and night continued unmercifully. After a few weeks the minister felt that Mary was suffering from sleep deprivation and offered to let the girl spend the night at his house with himself and his wife. Mary's parents agreed, hoping it would bring their daughter some peace.

Sometime during the night, the minister woke up to the sound of the bed in the guest room, where Mary was sleeping, shaking rapidly. Even when the minister grabbed the bed and tried to hold it still, the shaking continued without interruption. The minister then suggested that she try to sleep in a chair, but after just a few minutes the chair began to scoot a few inches across the floor. The minister suggested that Mary raise her legs so her full weight would hold the chair in place, but the chair continued to scoot across the floor and slam into a wall. Then it unceremoniously tilted and deposited her gently on the floor.

During all the events that took place that night, the minister noticed that the entire time Mary appeared to be in some kind of a trance-like state and she made no effort to jump out of the bed or the chair when the activity started—even though she'd had ample opportunity to do so.

After that night, the minister suggested that Mary be put into the hospital for medical tests and a psychological examination. Her parents readily agreed and Mary spent a mere four days in the hospital. During that time, she began to act wildly and would scream the words, "Go to St. Geneva" (location changed). According to some reports, those same words appeared as scratches on her skin; however, it's unclear if Mary did this to herself, or if it was due to some paranormal force.

Thinking that Mary could benefit from a trip, her parents took her to St. Geneva, where they stayed with relatives. The girl's condition worsened and a dispute broke out between her parents and relatives about who to call in—a Catholic priest or a Lutheran minister. A compromise of sorts was reached and they called in a Jesuit.

The Jesuit Father visited Mary and performed prayers and a blessing, but it didn't take long for him to realize she had gone far beyond a demonic infestation, so he called in a priest.

After the priest evaluated Mary's condition, he sought permission from the bishop to perform an exorcism in an effort to save the poor girl. The bishop and archbishop agreed and the exorcism was scheduled.

As the exorcism dragged on, Mary would cough up phlegm and constantly drool. Painful and bloody welts and scratches would rise up on her body. Mary almost constantly cursed, spat, and physically attacked the exorcists, showing an extraordinary amount of strength for a woman her size.

It would appear that the demon left her exhausted body, only to rise up and once again begin to assault the priests both verbally and physically.

During one of Mary's short lapses of relief, the priests moved her to a secure location in a hospital and resumed the exorcism. While it's unclear how many people participated in the exorcisms, the priests were relentless in their pursuit of ridding Mary's body of the demonic entity.

A few days later the priests wanted to move Mary to the church in hopes that getting her on sacred ground would give them the edge over the relentless demon. However, she wasn't allowed to enter the church for fear that her mere presence could desecrate the sanctity of the chapel. Instead, she was taken to the rectory where she continued to vomit, struggle against the exorcists, and fling obscenities at all who entered.

A baptism took place, followed by a communion that Mary could actually participate in and successfully complete. After several weeks of relapses, her condition continued to improve. After almost thirty exorcisms over a period of about six weeks, the exorcism was deemed to be successful. Some people who were either in the room or in the building where Mary was being housed swore they heard a loud sound like thunder right before the demon left her body. Mary returned to her parents and led a normal life up until her death from old age.

Even though Mary is deceased, the debate about her case rages on in some circles. Some people believe that mental illness could have been to blame for her condition as she never exhibited many of the classic signs of demonic possession, including speaking in languages that were foreign to her.

However, others close to what happened swear that Mary was indeed possessed by a demon as there was no other possible explanation. These people believe that, had it not been for the priests and others who never gave up until they were successful, the demonic entity inside of Mary might have killed the young woman.

The Story Behind the Movie: The Exorcism of Emily Rose

While the name of this woman is readily available on the Internet and through other sources, I've changed her name in this book out of respect, because even though she is deceased, there is no need for this woman to be victimized yet again. For the purposes of this book, I will use the name that was used in the movie: Emily Rose.

Emily was born in Bavaria, West Germany, into a family of devout Catholics. She had three sisters, although one of them died at an early age of kidney disease.

Another one of her sisters was an illegitimate daughter of her mother's. This, of course, due to the times and culture, brought shame and scandal to the family and Emily felt it was her duty to pay penance for her mother's sin. Therefore, Emily was quite withdrawn from others in an attempt at repentance for her mother.

When Emily turned sixteen, she experienced an extremely violent seizure and tests revealed she suffered from a form of epilepsy that was centered in the temporal lobe in her brain. She was given medication to control her disease and attempted to live a normal life.

Emily became hypersensitive and sometimes during mass at church she would be overcome with emotion. Her parents believed, with her temperament, she would make a good school teacher, and she was sent away to a special school to continue her studies.

However, Emily continued to suffer seizures and experienced a blackout while at that school. She felt as if she was paralyzed, short of breath, and unable to control her bladder.

She was taken to see a neurologist, but there wasn't a medication that seemed to have the desired effect of controlling the seizures. Because of this, Emily became increasingly depressed and withdrawn. She was finally sent to a psychiatric hospital for treatment.

Just as with her epilepsy, nothing the doctors did seemed to alleviate her depressive state and Emily soon developed other problems, such as pleurisy, pneumonia, tuberculosis, heart problems, and circulatory problems—to the point she was placed in a sanitarium.

Emily also began complaining about having specific visions while she was praying. An electroencephalogram (EEG) revealed she had abnormal brain waves and she was again put on another medication. However, it did little to stop the visions that plagued her.

She also began to complain about hearing voices. They started out as if in the distance at first, but soon they made themselves understood as if someone was standing right next to her.

While in the hospital, Emily experienced her first demonic vision while she was deep in prayer. She saw a cruel face that scared her tremendously. In fear of seeing that face again, Emily became afraid to pray and only did it sparingly.

However, the vision of the face made her think that maybe she had a demon inside of her causing all of her problems and she had frequent thoughts of suicide.

After she returned home from the sanitarium, she continued to hear voices that often urged her to do certain things, and at other times threatened her. Although she resumed her studies, her grades were not good and she became increasingly despondent.

Her family became concerned when Emily began to show an intense aversion to religious places and objects. Emily even refused to drink water from a holy spring while on a religious pilgrimage. She also refused to enter a Catholic shrine, claiming that the soil was making her feet burn, and she refused to wear the medal of a saint her father purchased for her, saying that she felt like she couldn't breathe whenever she wore the necklace.

A friend of the family noticed that Emily had developed an unusual and unpleasant smell that seemed to linger around her, and this friend suggested that the family consult a priest.

Emily's family consulted many priests but were told time and again that they should send her back to the hospital for more treatment. They were also informed that unless they could prove Emily was possessed by a demon, the priests wouldn't go to the Church to ask for permission to perform an exorcism. The family became more and more discouraged as they were rapidly dismissed by many of the priests they talked to.

One priest, however, Father Patrick, decided to investigate the family's claims out of curiosity. He met with Emily several times and soon became convinced that she was being possessed by a demonic entity.

Her mother felt the same way, claiming that Emily's eyes had turned black and her hands resembled paws and claws more than human hands.

Father Patrick wrote an extremely passionate and convincing letter to the bishop, begging him to give permission to have an exorcism performed in an attempt to help Emily.

Eventually the bishop agreed, although he did stipulate that the exorcism must be conducted in secret. The bishop sent another priest, Father Stephen, to assist Father Patrick with the exorcism. Little did the priests know, as they began the Rites of Exorcism, that it would span a period of ten months and result in the death of Emily Rose.

As the priests began the exorcism Emily claimed that she was possessed by many spirits. She became so desperate to gain some type of control over the demons that possessed her that she began to flog, or beat, herself to the point that she couldn't stand by herself—someone had to hold her in an upright position. No one forced her to do this. It was her choice and she believed it would help release the grip the demons had upon her and make it easier for the exorcists to get them out of her body.

It took three strong men to hold Emily down while the priests performed an exorcism. She kicked, screamed, and attempted to bite the men on more than one occasion.

As hard as the priests worked to remove the demons from Emily, everything they did only seemed to worsen her condition. She would frequently urinate and defecate on the floor and then drink her own urine, she would growl and snarl like a wild animal, and in an extreme fit she spent an entire two days under a table barking like a dog. This behavior scared her family to the point that they wouldn't go near her, and most of the time she was left alone with the priests.

At one point after numerous exorcisms the priests thought they had finally won, as one by one they got the demons to leave Emily's body. Their victory was short-lived, however, as another demon came forth and growled at the priests. He referred to himself simply as "I" and stated that he'd been with Emily all along, hiding in the shadows of the other demons. He told the priests that the demons had "pulled a fast one" on the priests.

The demon then announced one day that his real name was Judas and he'd returned to Emily immediately after the priests thought he'd been exorcised. He later recanted that statement and announced that he was Lucifer himself.

Even though the priests were performing the Rites of Exorcism at least once or twice a week, nothing they did seemed to have an effect on the demons that had ahold of Emily. The exorcisms went on for months and it's estimated that at least sixty-seven exorcisms were performed.

During this time, Emily chipped her teeth from biting a wall, put her head through a pane of glass without suffering any injuries, and only slept one or two hours a day. In addition, as fast as the priests were casting out the demons, others would show up to take their place and generally refused to communicate with the priests or give their names.

As the days and months dragged on, the priests began to think that Emily was suffering from a "penance possession," which is when someone atones for someone else's sins, perhaps those of her mother for having an illegitimate child.

The priests knew that a penance possession was one of the most difficult things to treat and they continued to perform exorcisms up to three or more times a week. The priests were exhausted by their efforts. Emily even tried to perform an exorcism on herself and declined to see a doctor.

As the ordeal neared the end, Emily refused to eat and became extremely thin—a mere shell of the person she'd once been. It was as though she had resigned herself to the fact that she was going to die, and perhaps controlling her death was the only measure of control Emily thought she had over the demons that were ravaging her.

After approximately ten months of exorcisms Emily died at her home. At the time of her death she weighed only sixty-eight pounds. The autopsy revealed the cause of death to be malnutrition, dehydration, and pneumonia.

The night before she died, she'd asked the priests for absolution and told her mother that she was extremely scared. Emily was also running a very high fever.

Soon after Emily's death an investigation began to determine the exact circumstances that caused the young woman to die. Many people didn't want to believe that Emily died because of demonic possession, because to them that would mean that evil could beat the good. Instead, some people chose to believe that she had sacrificed herself and people made pilgrimages to pray at her grave. The state concluded that the two priests could have intervened and prevented Emily's death. The priests were then put on trial for negligent homicide.

During the trial, the court was forced to endure the horror of listening to the forty-seven exorcisms that had been recorded. On the tapes they heard Emily growling and snarling. At one point it sounded as if two demons were arguing with each other, as there were two distinct voices coming out of Emily's mouth. The court also heard her talking in ancient languages and relaying information she had no way of knowing.

Many pictures were shown in the courtroom of Emily. Some depicted her with sunken eyes, bruises, and weeping sores that covered most of her small body. As a result of Emily's self-harming activities both her knees were broken.

The priest's attorneys argued that the priests had done everything they could to save Emily, and that in death she was finally free of the demons that had tormented her for years. The attorneys also argued that their work was within the law and that citizens had a right to religious freedom.

The court found that the priests had not gone far enough to try to save Emily and they were found guilty of manslaughter. They received a sentence of six months in jail and three months of probation, but their jail sentence was suspended.

The bizarre case of Emily Rose didn't end with her death or the end of the trial. Two years later, her family had her body exhumed, because when Emily died she'd been buried in a cheap coffin and the family felt the need to bury her properly—at least that was the official story.

A nun had come forward to the family and said that Emily was communicating from beyond the grave and that she had died to pay penance for her country, its youth, and the priests, and that she wanted to be re-buried before the trial started.

The nun also said that Emily told her that her body would not be decayed, but would prove the existence of God, demons, other spiritual beings, eternal life, resurrection, and the existence of hell.

The people who believed that Emily was possessed claimed that her body didn't show the amount of decay one would expect after such a long period of time, while medical experts said that the amount of decay was be what one would expect and advised the family not to view the remains because of the level of decomposition.

The priests that performed the exorcism were not allowed to view Emily's body and some believe this was because they would know that the body had not decayed as much as it should have. No matter what Emily's body looked like, the entire event was a media circus and caused quite a stir in the community.

Emily's body was tenderly placed in an oak coffin lined with tin and reburied in her final resting place.

In a strange turn of events a fire occurred at Emily's family's home. While the fire was ruled an arson, there are those who believe that it was started by something evil that was starting once again to invade Emily's family.

Life after Demons

As the demonic encounters in this book clearly show, demons are very powerful entities capable of things that seem unimaginable. Many of the victims of a demonic attack or possession don't make it out alive.

Some people could argue that many people in the stories didn't die at the hands of a demon, but at the hands of religious fanatics, mental illness, and, in some cases, cultural beliefs. It's a valid argument for many of the cases you've read about in this book; however, who's to say that a demon wasn't at play in those cases as well—they just got someone else to do their dirty work? The truth is, we'll never really know for sure.

It makes one wonder … What is life like after the demon is gone? Do things just fall back into order and life goes on? I would have to say, from personal experience, for the most part the answer is no.

Yes, life goes on, but things are never the same after coming out the other side of a demonic encounter. A person is forever changed spiritually and psychologically. What those changes exactly are differs from person to person and a lot depends on the severity of the interaction with the demonic entity. By interaction I mean demonic oppression, repression, infestation, and possession.

In many cases, your entire belief system has been rocked to the core and it takes a lot of time to process what's happened to you. There are some things you can do to help you recover as much as possible after your life has been touched by a demon.

Clean House

I mean this literally and figuratively. Figuratively speaking, one of the first steps to moving on after a demonic interaction is to do a complete analysis of how the demon entered your life in the first place. Once a demon has been allowed into your life it may be looking for a way to come back, so you need to close the point of entry to prevent that from happening.

Earlier in this book I outlined the various ways a demon can enter your life, and I won't reiterate them here; however, once you know what door opened to let the demon in, you need to make appropriate changes to make yourself a less attractive target. For example, was it drawn to you because you're surrounded by negativity, such as an abusive relationship, drug use, improper use of a Ouija board and/or other occult tools, or alcohol abuse? If so, then make appropriate changes and cut those bad habits out of your life.

Literally, clean house. Demons and other negative entities thrive on chaos. Clean out closets, get rid of clutter, and give your house a good cleaning and keep it clean. In other words—get your home in order.

Fight the Fear

I personally know the fear that can set in after having your life invaded by a demonic entity and I know how hard it is to let go of that fear—but you have to and here's why.

Fear is your enemy when dealing with most negative entities. They feed on it and in some cases your fear can make them more powerful. I understand that you may be constantly looking over your shoulder, jumping at any little noise and constantly feeling as if you may be barely functioning due to the paralysis of fear, but let it go. I know what you're thinking: Easier said than done. I can't argue with that—it's hard, but you can do it.

When I came out on the other side of the demonic infestation I experienced, I was filled with fear. I had to sit down with myself and have a serious discussion on how to overcome it. What I decided to do was get back into a daily routine—minus any negative activities that allowed the demon to enter my life in the first place. Then I decided that I wasn't going to let this entity have any power or control over me ever again.

I didn't get angry, because anger is a negative emotion and could let the demon right back into my life, Instead, I became determined and purpose-driven. Every time a thought came into my head about the demon, or something happened that made me think the demon was still around, I pushed that thought or notion out of my head. I pushed forward and made conscious choices. I didn't let my past experience with the demon influence my decisions. You can do the same thing. It does take time, but pretty soon it just becomes a habit.

Deal with the Depression

Some people experience some type of depression after their life has been touched by a demonic entity and aren't sure what to do about it. Many people become apprehensive about going into therapy. They're afraid that a therapist won't believe the experience they've been through with the demon. Unfortunately, in many cases, the concern in this area may be well-founded, but it doesn't mean a person shouldn't try therapy if they believe it will help them battle their depression. In addition, a person shouldn't be afraid of taking antidepressants if prescribed by their doctor. As long as a drug is not being abused, it should be fine.

It's important that a person suffering from depression after a demonic encounter get help, because the depression itself could be enough to let the demon back into that person's life while their defenses are down.

No matter what method(s) a person chooses to help them recover from a demonic entity, they should also employ one or more of the protection methods listed in the next chapter. Or, alternatively, come up with a personal protection method that works for them.

Don't Be Afraid to Ask for Help

However someone chooses to recover from their life being affected by a demon, they should never be afraid to ask for help. Whether that help comes in the form of a priest or other member of clergy, a good therapist, a trusted friend or family member, and/or a properly trained and experienced person who is knowledgeable about the paranormal, help is available. Having a good support system can be vital in a person's recovery.

HOW TO PROTECT YOURSELF FROM NEGATIVE ENTITIES

If you're like me and many other ghost hunters, if you run around looking for evidence of ghosts and spirits, eventually you're going to run into a demon or other type of negative entity. My team and I employ various methods to protect ourselves, such as prayers, amulets, crystals, and/or calling down a divine white light. So how can you protect yourself if you run into a demon or other form of negative phantom? By using the same methods my team and I use, plus some we don't. Not that the ones we don't use won't work, because they will, it's just that everyone has to find what works for them and their own personal belief system. It's just like anything else, if you don't believe one hundred percent in what you're doing, it won't work.

So take some time and go through the different methods I've outlined below—don't be afraid to experiment a little with them and find the one that you're most comfortable with and use it whenever you feel it's necessary.

Prayers of Protection

You've heard the expression, "Never underestimate the power of prayer"? Well, in many cases it's very true. Prayer can be very powerful no matter what Divine Power you believe in.

Some of the more powerful protection prayers for Christians come from the Holy Bible. They include Psalm 23 and Psalm 91.

Psalm 23

The Lord is my shepherd; I shall not want. He maketh me to lie down in green pastures; he leadeth me beside the still waters. He restoreth my soul, he leadeth me on the paths of righteousness for his name's sake. Yea, though I walk through the valley of the shadows of death; I will fear no evil: for thou art with me; thy rod and thy staff they comfort me. Thou preparest a table before me in the presence of mine enemies; thou anointest my head with oil; my cup runneth over. Surely goodness and mercy shall follow me all the days of my life; and I will dwell in the house of the Lord forever.

I'm sure most of you have heard or recited this verse at some time in your life but didn't realize that it was a protection prayer as well as a proclamation of faith in God and how he helps a person through their life.

It's important to realize that the passage about the shadow of death can be interpreted in many ways. When used as a protection prayer, we're talking about not only dark times in our lives, but fear and the belief that fear can kill you. When you release your fear, you are truly set free. If you're unafraid you can think clearly and logically deal with any situation, including a negative entity, with a clear mind and in control of the situation, instead of having the situation control you.

Psalm 91

In the New American Standard Bible, Pslam 91 reads as follows:

> He who dwells in the shelter of the Most High will rest in the shadow of the Almighty. I will say of the Lord, "He is my refuge and my fortress, my God in whom I trust. Surely he will save you from the fowler's snare and from the deadly pestilence. He will cover you with his feathers, and under his wings you will find refuge; his faithfulness will be your shield and rampart. You will not fear the terror of night, nor the arrow that flies by day, nor the pestilence that stalks in the darkness, nor the plague that destroys at midday. A thousand may fall at your side, ten thousand at your right hand, but it will not come near you. You will only observe with your eyes and see the punishment of the wicked. If you make the Most High your dwelling—even the Lord, who is my refuge—then no harm will befall you, no disaster will come near your tent. For he will command his angels concerning you to guard you in all your ways; they will lift you up in their hands, so that you will not strike your foot against a stone. You will tread upon the lion and the cobra, you will trample the great lion and the serpent. 'Because he loves me,' says the Lord, 'I will rescue him; I will protect him, for he acknowledges my name. He will call upon me, and I will answer him, I will be with him in trouble,

I will deliver him and honor him. With long life I will satisfy him and show him my salvation."

This entire bible verse is about protection. Take notice of the words "refuge," "guard," and "shield." The use of those words lets Christians know that if you have faith in the Lord, then you shall be protected.

This verse talks about darkness and pestilence—while these words can be associated with many things, when you're asking for protection from demonic or negative entities these words take on a clear meaning.

St. Patrick's Breastplate
It is said this prayer was written by St. Patrick in Ireland and is contained in the Book of Armagh. The entire prayer was later turned into a hymn and is quite long. When using this as a protection prayer against negative entities or energy, some people shorten the prayer. Since we're discussing protection, the shortened version appears here. The entire prayer can be found at: www.joyfulheart.com/stpatrick/breastplate.htm.

> I bind myself today. God's power to guide me, God's might to uphold me, God's wisdom to teach me, God's eye to watch over me, God's word to give me speech, God's hand to guide me, God's way to lie before me, God's shield to shelter me, God's host to secure me against the snares of demons, against the seduction of vices, against the lusts of nature, against everyone who meditates to injury to me, whether far or near, whether few or with many. Christ with me, Christ before me, Christ behind me, Christ

within me, Christ above me, Christ at my right, Christ at my left, Christ in the fort, Christ in the chariot seat, Christ in the stern. Christ in the heart of everyone who thinks of me, Christ in the mouth of everyone who speaks to me, Christ in the eye that sees me, Christ in every ear that hears me.

As you read through this prayer you can't help but notice how powerful the words are. While this is a general protection prayer and you can say it every day if you so choose, it also can provide good protection against negative or demonic entities.

Prayers to St. Michael, the Archangel

One of the prayers to St. Michael is what I use for protection—not only on a daily basis, but when I'm on a ghost hunt, or in a place where I feel negative energy. This particular prayer was promulgated by Pope Leo XIII. This is the short version, the longer version may be found at: http://www.traditioninaction .org/religious/b009rpMichael.htm.

St. Michael the Archangel defend us in battle. Be our defense against the wickedness and snares of the devil. May God rebuke him, we humbly pray. And do thou, O Prince of the heavenly host, by the power of God, thrust into hell Satan and other evil spirits who prowl about the world for the ruin of souls. Amen.

You can also use the protection prayer below as found at www .pwsm-ri.org; however, while it is a protection prayer, it is also a prayer for everyday use.

Dear St. Michael the Archangel, protect us, both body and soul, from the Evil One, his followers, and anyone who would approach us with malicious intent. Protect us, our bodies, and our cars, as we travel about in our daily activities. Protect us our bodies, our home, our property and possessions from all demonic retaliation. Father, if there are unholy Angels in, on, near, or around us. We nail and hold them fast and silence them. We decommission, bind, and encapsulate them through the Power of Shed Blood of Your Son, Jesus Christ. We bring them up to your presence immediately, Lord, to deal with as you see fit. May you fill empty spaces and lonely places within us with your love and your light. Thank you, Father, in Jesus's name. Amen.

Protection Prayer by James Dillet Freeman

James Dillet Freeman, besides being a renowned poet, author, and speaker, was also a Unity minister and the protection prayer he wrote was one of two poems of his that was taken to the moon by the Apollo astronauts. Buzz Aldrin had a copy with him when he landed on the moon, and in 1971 a microfilm copy containing Freeman's poem "I Am There" was left on the moon by astronaut James B. Irwin on the Apollo XV mission.

This small but powerful protection spell was written by Freeman in 1940 when WWII was raging on and people were requesting a protection prayer.

It is also one of the prayers several of our team members use. The prayer goes like this:

The light of God surrounds us; The love of God enfolds
us; The power of God protects us; The presence of God
watches over us; Wherever we are, God is!

White Light Prayer

For all my friends who aren't Christian, the White Light protection prayer is a nondenominational and spiritual prayer that you
may choose to use in many situations. While there are many
versions of this prayer on the Internet and in books, they are all
rather similar to the one below:

We ask the Divine Light Force of our beings, our Higher
Selves, to clear this space of all that is not of the light, and
Protection against all that is negative forces in all possible
dimensions and timelines, here & now, with harm to none.

Sacred Objects

Protective amulets and other sacred objects have been used by
civilizations since ancient times to defend a person against demonic entities and certain spirits. This practice continues on even
today in certain religions and belief systems. The key to choosing
what works for you depends solely upon your personal religious
and/or spiritual views.

You can also have objects blessed and place them in your
home. Some people choose to just place a blessed object in one
room of their house, while others choose to have many objects
blessed and place them in every room of their home; the choice
is yours.

Some of the most common and a few uncommon sacred objects are listed below. This list is by no means all-inclusive.

Medal of St. Benedict

St. Benedict of Italy lived between A.D. 480–543 and is considered by many to be the father of Western Monasticism. His "Rule of St. Benedict" is believed to be the foundation for the organization of several religious orders. For a three-year period of his life he lived as a hermit in a cave and was quite renowned for his holiness in the surrounding communities. A group came to him one day after their own abbot died and asked him to take the deceased abbot's place. Some of the monks didn't agree with this choice and attempted to poison St. Benedict with wine and bread. However, their plan failed when St. Benedict made the sign of the cross over the food and could instantly detect that it was filled with poison. He spilled out the cup and called upon a raven to carry off the bread.

The medal, still widely used today, was approved by Pope Benedict XIV in 1741. Before that, it's believed it was first in the shape of a cross. Pope Leo IX carried the cross with him and believes it was the St. Benedict cross that prevented him from dying of a snakebite. It's widely held that Pope Leo IX in 1049 was the first to convert the cross into medal form.

The Jubilee Medal was first made in 1880 to commemorate the fourteenth centenary of St. Benedict's birth and the Archabbey of Monte Cassino is the only abbey that has the right to make this particular medal, as St. Benedict's order was first established there.

The regular St. Benedict's Medal is only slightly different than the Jubilee Medal in that it doesn't contain the words "Ejus in obitu nostro praesentia muniamus," which means, "May we at our death be fortified by his presence," and a few other minor changes.

This fact, however, does not make a normal St. Benedict's Medal any less powerful than the Jubilee Medal.

Some people refer to the St. Benedict's Medal as the "devil-chasing medal" because of its perceived power against evil and Satan himself. In fact, on the back of the medal are the words "Vade Retro Satana, Nunquam Suade Mihi Vana-Sunt Mala Quae Libas, Ipse Venena Bibas," which means, "Begone, Satan, do not suggest to me they vanities—evil are the things thou profferest, drink thy own poison." The back of the medal also contains the words "Crux Sacra Sit Mihi Lux," that mean, "The Holy Cross be my light," and the words "Non Draco Sit Mihi Dux," which translates to, "Let not the dragon be my guide." At the top of the cross on the back of the medal there is normally the word "Pax," which means peace, and the monogram HIS, which is Jesus.

The front of a normal medal contains the words "Crus Sancti Patris Benedicti," means, "Cross of the Holy Father Benedict." On the Jubilee Medal there is the additional language discussed above.

It's believed by many Christians that the St. Benedict Medal can guard against demonic and other hauntings, protect a person from evil spirits, from temptation, protect against thunderstorms, neutralize the effects of poison, ensure the healthy birth of children, a remedy for certain diseases, and protect from contagious disease, and convert sinners to the Catholic Church.

St. Benedict Medals can be used in a variety of different ways: They can be worn as a necklace, put on a rosary, or kept on your person, in your car, in the foundation of a building, and in the center of a cross.

Crosses and Crucifixes

The cross and crucifix have been symbols of Christianity for many years and are probably the most well-known and instantly recognizable of all religious symbols around the globe.

Both the cross and the crucifix are symbols to remind Christians and Catholics alike of the sacrifice that Jesus Christ made for humankind and have long been held as symbols of protection against evil.

While some people believe a cross and crucifix are the same thing, there are differences that are important to note. A cross is a plain T-shaped object, while a crucifix holds the body of Jesus as he was crucified on a cross. In other words, a cross can become a crucifix if it holds the body of Christ.

Generally, Catholics will use a crucifix, while many other Christians will use a cross. However, a crucifix or a cross may be used by all Christians regardless of their individual religion.

Many Christian religions encourage their parishioners to say prayers in front of the cross or crucifix, not just in the same room or church where they are placed. Many Christians hang a cross or crucifix above their doors, on walls, or displayed on tables in their homes as a symbol of their beliefs and for protection against evil.

If using a cross or crucifix for protection, whether it is to be worn as a necklace or other piece of jewelry or displayed in your home, you should have it blessed. You can ask a priest to bless them for you and many Catholic churches allow you to drop such items off to be blessed and then picked up once the blessing is complete. You could also ask your priest, minister, and/or reverend to bless them after Sunday services.

The Rosary

A rosary is used to keep count of a certain number of prayers that can be said daily by mostly people of the Catholic religion. Just like many religious symbols, they are only a tool and should be blessed by a priest and treated with reverence.

What's of interest to many people looking for protection from evil forces is that the Blessed Mary promised people in one specific prayer that the rosary can be a powerful armor against the forces of hell and that it will rid one of vices, decrease sin, and beat down heresies.

While the rosary is said daily by many Catholics and others, the rosary has also been adopted by some new-age thinkers as a powerful symbol of protection, among other things.

Some people might call this blasphemy and could probably make some strong arguments for their case. However, other people believe that God doesn't have a religion because religions are man-made, not created by God; therefore, they have the right to use whatever sacred objects give them comfort, protection, and fit in with their individual belief systems. These people believe that just because they aren't Catholic, doesn't in any way diminish the power or meaning of these objects, such as a rosary.

Holy Water and Exorcised Salt

Holy Water has been used for centuries and in many different religions to help protect and get rid of evil as well as in cleansing of spaces thought to have negative spirits and/or energy. In many religions it's also used to wash away impurities and sin.

Catholic Christian traditions have long held that Holy Water can be used to summon God's blessings on the people using the Holy Water and to give protection from all forms of evil. A symbol of baptism, Holy Water can be sprinkled upon people, places, and things.

While normally a priest will bless the Holy Water and make it available to his parishioners, many people don't realize you can bless your own Holy Water—if you're comfortable doing that.

One of the many blessings available for the Holy Water can be found in the Novus Ordo Book of Blessings and goes like this: "Blessed are you, Lord, Almighty God, who deigned to bless us in Christ, the living water of our salvation, and to reform us interiorly, grant that we who are fortified by the sprinkling or use of this water, the youth of the spirit being renewed by the power of the Holy Spirit, may walk always in the newness of life." You then make the sign of the cross over the water.

Sometimes Holy Water is mixed with either plain salt or exorcised salt. This is done to protect those who use the salty Holy Water from sickness, sinning, and being influenced by a demonic force. Some priests choose to use Holy Water mixed with salt for house blessings and use pure Holy Water for exorcisms and other rites, and vice versa.

One of the prayers to exorcise salt is as follows:

"O salt, creature of God, I exorcise you by the living God, by the true God, by the holy God, by the God who ordered you to be poured into the water by Eliseo the Prophet so that its life-giving powers might be restored. I exorcise you so that you may become a means of salvation for believers, that you may bring health of soul and body to all who make use of you, and that you may put to flight and drive away from the places where you are sprinkled every apparition, villainy, and turn of devilish deceit, and every unclean spirit, adjured by Him who will come to judge the living and the dead and the world by fire. Amen. Almighty and everlasting God, we humbly implore Thee, in Thy immeasurable kindness and love, to bless and sanctify this salt which Thou did create and give over to the use of mankind, so that it may become a source of health for the minds and bodies of all who make use of it, and may rid whatever touches or sprinkles of all uncleanness and protect it from every assault of evil spirits. Through our Lord, Jesus Christ, Thy Son, Who lives and reigns with Thee in the unity of the Holy Spirit, God, forever and ever. Amen."

Our paranormal team uses Holy Water extensively in our cleansing of our client's homes or places of business and worship. As is common practice when using Holy Water, we dip our finger in the Holy Water and make the sign of the cross when we are doing our cleansing ritual.

Just as there are many prayers one could use to make Holy Water and to exorcise salt, there are just as many ways to use them. Our team uses Holy Water mixed with a little exorcised salt in our house cleansing rituals. The one we use is below, but feel free to explore other options and find the cleansing and/or house blessings that you're the most comfortable with and use them as often as you feel it's necessary.

Just like when I smudge a house, I open a window in the last room of the house I'm going to cleanse. This is so any negative energies that are trying to escape the cleansing have an easy exit to the outside. I start at the farthest point away from that open window and at the highest point of the house, generally the attic, and then work my way down.

In each room I start at the back of the room and, after dipping my finger in the Holy Water and as I make the sign of the cross on the wall, I say: "Dear Lord, please cleanse and bless this home. Dispel any negative energy and replace it with your divine white light. I cleanse this space in the name of our Father, Son, and Holy Spirit."

I repeat this on every window, wall, and door in the building. When doing the doors, make sure you do both the inside and outside of the door. Work your way through the house until the last room you have to cleanse is the one with the open window.

When you get to that room, start at the entrance to the room and work your way around the room until the last thing you need to cleanse is the open window. Once that's done, close the window.

The prayer our team uses is printed above, but feel free to use whatever prayer, bible verse, incantation, or saying means something to you. As I've said before, if you don't believe one hundred percent in what you're doing, it won't work.

Other Talismans

Throughout history, almost every culture and civilization used some type of talisman or symbol to ward off evil forces, such as negative entities, curses, hexes, and the like. Many of these symbols are still used today for the same purpose and you can employ them to help protect you against demons and other dark entities. Remember, it doesn't matter what you use as long as you believe it works.

Pyramid

In some cultures it's believed that by placing a pyramid under your bed you will be protected against evil spirits, psychic attacks, and nightmares. Pyramids are also said to aid in healing, getting rid of headaches and insomnia, and helping a person rid themselves of unhealthy habits.

Scarab

The wearing of a scarab symbol, whether it be on a necklace or other piece of jewelry, is believed to ward off evil spirits and can bring good luck and renewal in your life.

Scorpion

Just as many people are repulsed by scorpions and flee from them in fear, negative and evil energies feel exactly the same way. Wearing a piece of jewelry adorned with a scorpion will assist you in protecting yourself against evil and protect you from any enemies. I personally have a necklace with a scorpion amulet on it and wear it when going on a ghost hunt or if I'm going to be in a large crowd of people.

Unicorn

To most people the unicorn represents purity and is an ancient symbol that represents chastity. However, a unicorn is also a powerful symbol of protection against evil forces. Unicorns are also believed to increase sexual magnetism and make the person who wears them more fertile.

Four-Leaf Clover

A four-leaf clover is thought by many to be one of the most powerful natural talismans available. Many Christians view a four-leaf clover as a symbol that is sacred to the Holy Trinity. Druid priests would use them to protect themselves against any evil that may be lurking about.

Using Crystals for Protection

Crystals have been used for centuries by humankind to assist them in their daily lives in various ways. For our purpose, however, we will focus only on some of the many crystals that can aid in protection against evil spirits, demons, and other dark forces.

Choosing Your Crystals

There are many ways to choose a crystal. Once you know what type of crystal you're looking for and set out to purchase it, selecting the right crystal is relatively easy.

Say for example you want to buy a turquoise crystal: When you're at the store, hold your hand palm down about an inch or so over the various turquoise crystals. The right one for you will practically leap into your hand. I can't explain how this works, but I know it works.

Other people will look over the crystals and pay attention to which ones they feel drawn to. They will then hold each of those crystals in their hand and decide which one they feel more comfortable with.

Whichever of these or other methods you use to select your crystals is fine as generally you will end up with the ones you were meant to have.

Cleansing and Charging your Crystals

As with any crystal, it's important to cleanse it and charge it with your intent before you use it. The crystals you buy were probably handled by countless people before they got to you, and quite possibly absorbed some of those people's energies—something you don't want. That's why this step is so important.

To cleanse your crystals you will need a bowl of warm water and some sea salt. You can use blessed salt, exorcised salt, Kosher sea salt, or any other type of sea salt. I use Kosher sea salt, but whatever type of sea salt you decide to use is up to your personal preference.

Put some warm water in the bowl and add the sea salt, stir until the salt is pretty dissolved, then add your crystals. There should be enough warm water in the bowl to totally cover the crystals. Let the crystals soak in the salted water for twenty-four hours.

Then take the crystals out of the water and pat dry with a soft cloth or paper towels.

To charge your crystals you once again have a choice. You can charge them in sunlight or moonlight. I prefer moonlight, but sunlight works just as well—again, personal preference.

Before you place your crystals outside in the sunlight or moonlight, you should hold each crystal individually and let it absorb your energy. This is the time when you also want to charge the crystal with your intent. For example, since the crystals I use are for protection, I hold each crystal in my hand and say, "I charge you not only with my individual energy, but with the intent that you will protect me from any evil, demonic entities, and all negative energies."

Once I've done this with each and every crystal, I set them outside to be charged in the light of preferably a full or new moon.

When this last step is completed, your crystal is ready for use. However, you should cleanse and recharge them about once a month depending on how much you use the crystal. If you use your crystals almost every day, you should cleanse and charge them every two weeks. If you use your crystal once a month or so, then you can cleanse and charge it every other month.

Different Protection Crystals

While there are many different crystals you can use for protection against negative energies, some of my personal favorites are listed below. Again, this list is not all-inclusive.

Plancheite

Plancheite is a copper-based mineral that has crystal properties. Its color ranges from light blue to almost turquoise. It is generally used by people to bring them courage and strength during particularly stressful times. However, it's also used as a powerful protection against all types of negative energy.

Jet

Jet, sometimes referred to as black amber or lignite, is actually driftwood that has fossilized into a form of lignite coal. Some jet mined in Whitby, England, dates back to about 180 million years ago—which would be during the Jurassic era.

Jet can be polished, which gives it an extremely shiny appearance; that's why it's so popular for jewelry and has even been used as beads for rosaries.

Its protection properties are extremely strong and can protect a person from all types of negative energies and evil.

Because jet absorbs all the negative energy it comes into contact with, it should be cleansed and recharged after each wearing.

Black Obsidian

Black obsidian is created when lava is cooled very quickly into volcanic glass. It is considered to be an extremely powerful stone and should be used with great care and mindfulness.

As a form of protection, black obsidian is closely tied to certain types of spirits or protectors that watch over us. Black obsidian was used in the Middle Ages to ward off negative and evil entities.

A lot like jet, black obsidian will absorb negative energies and negative emotions. Therefore, it should be cleansed and recharged on a very regular basis.

Other Crystals

Here are a few other crystals and gems that are said to ward off evil: amber, garnet, lapis lazuli, onyx, pearls, topaz, and turquoise, just to name a few.

Smudging

Not unlike the use of incense throughout Asia and Europe to ward off negative energies, Native Americans have been using dried herbs to do exactly the same thing. It's a practice that dates back thousands of years.

Traditionally sage and sweet grass are used in the smudging ritual. The sage is to dispel any negative energy and the sweet grass is to attract positive energy. While some people burn these herbs in a small bowl, smudge sticks are available that make the process a little more convenient.

In addition, for hundreds of years people have been burning various dried herbs and other plants because of the usefulness of the smoke it creates. Smoke itself is a very strong symbol in many religions and belief systems. Smoke has been and still is used to get rid of insects and prevent certain diseases.

Smoke is also used in many religious circles because of the belief that the smoke is going up towards heaven and it carries the prayers and wishes of mankind to God.

When used in the smudging ritual, it's the smoke that can creep into every nook and cranny to rid your home or place of business of negative energy and replace it with positive energy. The ritual itself is very easy to perform and anyone can smudge their own space, as it's not unlike the ritual used for a house cleansing/blessing.

How to Smudge Your Space

First plan your route. You're going to want to go from the highest point in your home, such as an attic, to the lowest—i.e., basement—and then back to the first floor. Open a window in the room on the main level of your home that you plan to smudge last—this gives the negative energy an exit out of your space.

You can use either loose dried sage and sweet grass or a smudge stick—I prefer a smudge stick because it's easier to use. I also use a large feather, such as a hawk's feather, to fan the smoke from the smudge stick where I want it, but you can use your hand and accomplish the same purpose.

Before you begin, plan what you want to say as your smudging. It can be a prayer, a blessing, a mantra, anything positive that you feel comfortable with and that you feel gives you some sort of protection. Personally I use the White Light Prayer that I talked about earlier in this chapter, but use what works for you.

I always start in the attic of a home and work my way from the farthest point in the attic back to the attic stairs. Make sure that the smoke from the smudge stick gets into every single area—especially the corners. As you fan the smoke, keep saying the passage you've selected.

Working your way through the house, go to the room farthest away from the room with the open window and systematically go room to room. Start in the back of the room farthest away from the door and work your way out of the room. Then do the basement if the home has one.

When you get to the last room you're going to work in reverse and start smudging at the doorway and work your way to the open window. Once you've finished, close the window.

I smudge my home about once a month, but you should smudge as often as you feel is necessary.

Incense

Not unlike smudging, incense has been used by different cultures and civilizations for hundreds if not thousands of years. There are now hundreds of different scents and many people believe that each aroma holds special properties and assists us with various situations or desires in our lives. In addition, it's not uncommon for one kind of incense to assist us in more than one way. For the purpose of this book, however, I will only discuss some of the incense aromas that deal with the type of protection needed to ward off evil entities and negative energies. While this list is not all-inclusive, it is made up of some of my favorite incenses used for protection.

Basil
Basil has long been thought to protect against evil entities. It can also be used to increase your concentration, happiness, confidence, decisiveness, and integrity.

Clove
If you want to get rid of negative energy, attract money, and improve your memory, you may want to try clove incense. It has a very strong aroma and contains many good properties to assist you with your life.

Dragon's Blood
One of my personal favorites! I burn a dragon's blood incense stick any chance I get. It's very good at getting rid of negative energy and evil entities. When burned with other incense, it's believed the magical powers of dragon's blood incense increases dramatically.

Frankincense
I use frankincense incense on ghost hunts almost exclusively. I also use it blended with myrrh incense. Frankincense has a remarkable fragrance and helps get rid of negative energy.

Ginger Root

For centuries people have burned ginger root and/or ginger root incense to keep dark entities away from them and to be protected from all types of evil.

Myrrh

Myrrh has many positive properties and is often used for purification purposes as well as for banishing evil. It was used extensively in ancient Egypt as offerings to their gods and goddesses, particularly Isis and Ra.

Pine

Pine incense has many uses. It can be used to banish evil and supernatural specters. It can also be used to attract money, for strength, and for cleansing and healing. In the past, pine was used to break curses or hexes and return them to whoever sent them—plus it smells incredible!

Sage

As discussed in the smudging section, dried sage is used to dispel negative energy. One could also use sage incense in a smudging ritual; however, I believe that dried sage might be a tad more powerful because it hasn't been processed into incense.

Vervain

Vervain has one clear purpose and that is to exorcise all types of dark energies, including all evil.

Wisteria

Besides emitting a very pleasant aroma, wisteria can be used to protect yourself and your family against all types of evil.

As you can clearly see, there are many ways to protect yourself from all types of negative entities. The choice is really how many of these you use and which ones you choose. When it comes down to it, you can't have too much protection, but don't go overboard with it either.

Personally I use prayers and different amulets. Which amulet I use on each particular day depends largely on where I'm going, what I'm doing, and how I feel that day.

I also smudge and bless my house with Holy Water on a monthly basis—more often if I've been in contact with what I perceive to be a negative entity.

The most important thing to take away from this chapter is to find what works for you and don't be afraid to experiment a bit with different types of protection until you get things exactly how you want them. Whether or not you have the items you choose to use blessed by a priest or other member of clergy is entirely up to you.

CONCLUSION

On our journey into the dark side of the paranormal we've learned about negative entities, including demons and other creatures that linger in the shadows waiting for a chance to prey upon their next victim.

My research clearly shows that the majority of religions, cultures, and civilizations—whether ancient or modern—all have some type of rituals to get rid of negative spirits and demons. Whatever your personal belief system is, take precautions to protect yourself and guard against negative entities, such as demons, from entering your life.

Just because you may not personally believe demons exist doesn't mean that they don't or that you are immune to their ways, because you aren't. In fact, because you may not believe in them makes you an easy target for a demon to enter your life.

I used to believe that demons didn't exist until I found myself doing battle with one. I'm not here to convince you that demons exist; I just want you to be open to the possibility and take the proper precautions to protect yourself and your family.

We've learned that demonic entities cannot enter our lives unless we give them permission, because we, as humans, have free will. However, as clearly stated, demons tend to take things very literally and often trick us in various ways to get us to let them stay. Remember—not doing anything to get rid of a demon that could be impersonating a child, deceased love one, or other type of entity in our homes could be all the invitation a demon needs to move in.

Being in a negative environment and/or abusing drugs and alcohol can also lure these beings into our lives. Improper use of a Ouija board or other tools people may use to make contact with the spirit world can also allow a demon to enter your life.

When demons do enter your life, their behavior can also mimic the signs of a traditional haunting or "normal" ghostly behavior. In many cases it takes a trained investigator to distinguish between a demonic infestation and a spirit that once lived in human form. If you believe you might be dealing with a demonic entity, don't engage it in any way.

Here's where the conundrum comes in: Don't assume that every occurrence of paranormal activity can be attributed to a demon, but don't assume it's due to a ghost or spirit either. Just exercise caution and if you're not sure what type of phantom you're dealing with, find a qualified paranormal investigator who is.

As with any paranormal activity it's important to rule out any logical explanation for the activity occurring in your home. Don't jump to conclusions. Faulty wiring, loose pipes, critters in the attic or basement, and many more things can mimic paranormal activity, and in reality it can turn out to be nothing more than a home maintenance issue.

When dealing with a person who you believe may have fallen victim to a demon, be it in the form of oppression, repression, or possession, make sure they get to a doctor to have a full battery of tests done to rule out a medical cause for their behavior. They should also undergo a complete psychological exam as well to rule out any type of mental illness. Again—don't jump to conclusions.

The Catholic Rites of Exorcism can be an effective tool; however, due to the recent changes they are falling under some criticism from many of the exorcists themselves. But that's for the Catholic Church to sort out. While the Rites of Exorcism are available just about anywhere, I didn't include them in this book because they shouldn't be used by anyone who isn't properly trained to use them. In other words: Don't try this at home.

If an exorcism is performed incorrectly and doesn't dispel the demon, the demon or other negative entity is going to be extremely angry and could retaliate, making a bad situation even worse. You can protect yourself by using one of the many tools discussed in this book: protection prayers, amulets, talismans, Holy Water, smudging, crystals, incense, and exorcised salt. The most important lesson I want you to take away from the protection section of this book is to use whatever prayer, amulet, talisman, or other tool you feel most comfortable with and that you believe in one hundred percent. It can't be stated enough that no matter what you do, if you don't believe it will work, it won't work.

While you don't necessarily have to believe in demons to have them take over your life, you do have to believe in what you're doing to get rid of them once they're there. This is because when you're battling with a demon you are taking part in the highest form of spiritual warfare that exists. Some would even say that you're fighting for your very existence. These people would say that once a demon possesses your body, you cease to exist, or you exist in a place that you can't get out of. Maybe that's part of what hell is: being possessed and not able to reclaim your body or your life, but being forced to sit back and watch yourself and your family being destroyed by an entity you don't know how to fight.

In many of the stories in this book, there may or may not have been a demon present at all. In some of the stories it could have been simply the belief that a demon was present that caused them to behave the way they did.

There were a few stories that dealt with family members trying to exorcise what they perceived to be demons out of a loved one. Acts of violence? Yes. Did they act out of love? In many of the stories, you'd have to answer yes.

So then the real question is: Were those people misguided by their own beliefs or was there something more sinister at work in the background, such as a demon influencing their behavior? We'll never really know the answer to that question, but the question itself demonstrates the influence a demon can have on someone's life if they allow it.

If you're a religious or spiritual person, regardless of your religion, hang onto your faith. Take comfort in it. Seek solace and strength from it. When dealing with a demonic entity, your unwavering faith in whatever Divine Power you believe in could be one of the only things that can help you walk out of the darkness and back into the light. It's not any particular "religion" that can help you find your way out of the darkness and living hell caused by a demon, it's your faith in whatever deity you believe in that will see you through.

Of course, as always, I'm right there with you. If you have questions, need help, or just want to drop me an email about this book or my other books you can always email me at: debichestnut@yahoo.com.

BIBLIOGRAPHY

Aquinas and More. "Crucifixes and Crosses in the Home."
www.aquinasandmore.com. http://goo.gl/5EVPeu.
Accessed December 1, 2015.

Bancarz, Steven. spiritandsciencemetaphysics.com. www.spirit-
scienceandmetaphysics.com/7-best-tools-to-protect-yourself-
from-negative. Accessed July 1, 2015.

Brown, Nathan Robert. "How to Protect Yourself Against Demonic Spirits." Idiotsguide.com. www.idiotsguides.com/reli-
gion-and-spirituality/supernatural/how-to-protect-yourself-
against-demonic-spirits/. Accessed December 1, 2015.

California Paranormal Research Organization. "A Few White
Light Prayers of Protection." calpara.org/2013/01/15/a-
few-white-light-prayers-of-protection. Accessed December
1, 2015.

Carota, Father Peter. "Traditional Holy Water." Traditional-
CatholicPriest.com. www.traditionalcatholicpriest
.com/2013/04/.25/traditional-holy-water/. Accessed
November 1, 2015.

DemonSlayer.org. "Symptoms of Demonic Attack and Possession." www.demon-slayer.org/symptoms-of-demonic-attack/. Accessed December 1, 2015.

Diamond, Stephen, PhD. "Giving the Devil His Due: Exorcism, Psychotherapy, and the Possession Syndrome." Psychologytoday.com. https://www.psychologytoday.com/blog/evil-deeds/201008/giving-the-devil-his-due-exorcism-psychotherapy-and-the-possession-syndrome. Accessed December 1, 2015.

DifferenceBetween.com. "Difference Between Cross and Crucifix." www.differencebetween.com/difference-between-cross-and-vs-crucifix/. Accessed December 1, 2015.

Father X. "The New Rite of Exorcism." Fisheaters.com. www.fisheaters.com/forums/index.php?topic=1353620.0. Accessed December 1, 2015.

Foundation for Paranormal Research. "How to Protect Yourself and Others from Demononic Entities." www.foundationforparanormalresearch.org/protection.html. Accessed December 1, 2015.

Hambrose, H. "7 Things You Must Know About St. Benedict's Medal." St. Peter's List. www.stpeterslist.com/8560/8-things-you-must-know-about-st-benedicts-medal. Accessed December 1, 2015.

Hansen, Dr. Will. "Dealing with Demons." Believer's Web. www.believersweb.org/view.cfm?ID=598. Accessed December 1, 2015.

Harton, Robyn A. "Crystal Meanings and More: Jet." Crystalsandjewelry.com. www.meanings.crystalsandjewelry.com/jet. Accessed December 1, 2015.

Harton, Robyn A. "Crystal Meanings and More: Plancheite." Crystalsandjewelry.com. www.meanings.crystalsandjewelry .com/plancheite. Accessed December 1, 2015.

Heather. "Exorcisms that Have Ended in Death." Unsolved-mysteries.com. http://www.unsolvedmysteries.com/ usm81745.html. Accessed December 1, 2015.

Joyful Heart Renewal Ministries. "St. Patrick's Breastplate." www.joyfulheart.com/stpatrick/breastplate.htm. Accessed December 1, 2015.

Knight-Ridder Newspapers. "Exorcism Try Fatal, Police Say." *Baltimore Sun.* http://articles.baltimoresun.com/1995-03-17/news/1995076196_1_ha-jesus-christ-demons. Accessed January 4, 2016.

Kyodo. "Faith Healer to Hang for Killing Six Followers." *Japan Times.* http://www.japantimes.co.jp/news/2002/05/11/ national/faith-healer-to-hang-for-killing-six-followers/# .Vop5VVJc5j8. Accessed January 4, 2016.

Martin, Malachi. *Hostage to the Devil: The Possession and Exorcism of Five Contemporary Americans.* San Francisco: HarperOne, 1976.

McPhee, Michelle, and Corky Siemaszko. "Family Killed Her: Mom, Grandma Are Arrested in Girl's Poison Slay." *Daily News.* http://www.nydailynews.com/archives/news/ family-killed-cops-mom-grannby-arrested-girl-poison-slay-article-1.765363. Accessed January 4, 2016.

Monarch 13. "Amulets and Symbols of Protection." Hub Pages. http://hubpages.com/education/protection-symbols. Accessed December 1, 2015.

Praesidium of Warriors of St. Michael™. "Articles of Protection from Negative and Demonic Forces." http://pwsm-ri.org/Spiritual-Protection/Articles-of-Protection-From-Negative-and-Demonic-Forces.html. Accessed December 1, 2015.

Praesidium of Warriors of St. Michael™. "Protection Prayers." www.pwsm-ri.org/Spiritual-Protection/Protection-Prayers. Accessed December 1, 2015.

Ryfle, Steve. "Men to Be Tried in Exorcism Death." *Los Angeles Times*. http://articles.latimes.com/1996-08-08/local/me-32473_1_exorcism-death. Accessed January 4, 2016.

Spheres of Light. "Black Obsidian." Spheresoflight.com. www.spheresoflight.com.au/index.php?=crystals-blackobsidian. Accessed November 1, 2015.

Times Staff and Wire Report. "Mother Pleads Guilty in Beating Death of Girl." *Los Angeles Times*. http://articles.latimes.com/1997/oct/02/local/me-38478. Accessed January 4, 2016.

Tom's Domain. "Rosary Introduction." tomsdomain.com. www.tomsdomain.com/rosary. Accessed December 1, 2015.

Unity.org. "Prayer for Protection." www.unity.org/resources/articles/prayer-protection. Accessed December 1, 2015.

UPI. "Thai Mother Killed in Stingray Exorcism." *United Press International*. http://www.upi.com/Archives/1996/04/21/Thai-mother-killed-in-stingray-exorcism/8004830059200/. Accessed January 4, 2016.

The Witchy Way to Celebrate. "Incense Fragrance Meanings." https://www.facebook.com/notes/the-witchy-way-to-celebrate/incense-fragrance-meanings/120611068097468. Accessed December 1, 2015.

To Write to the Author

If you wish to contact the author or would like more information about this book, please write to the author in care of Llewellyn Worldwide Ltd. and we will forward your request. Both the author and publisher appreciate hearing from you and learning of your enjoyment of this book and how it has helped you. Llewellyn Worldwide Ltd. cannot guarantee that every letter written to the author can be answered, but all will be forwarded. Please write to:

Debi Chestnut
℅ Llewellyn Worldwide
2143 Wooddale Drive
Woodbury, MN 55125-2989

Please enclose a self-addressed stamped envelope for reply,
or $1.00 to cover costs. If outside the U.S.A., enclose
an international postal reply coupon.

Many of Llewellyn's authors have websites with additional information and resources. For more information, please visit our website at http://www.llewellyn.com.

IS YOUR HOUSE HAUNTED?

Poltergeists, Ghosts or Bad Wiring

Debi Chestnut

Is Your House Haunted?
Poltergeists, Ghosts or Bad Wiring
Debi Chestnut

A door slams shut by itself, pets are acting strangely, inexplicable smells and sounds are invading your home...and you're terrified. Is there a logical explanation, or do you have a real-life ghost on your hands?

There's no reason to live in fear. This no-nonsense beginner's guide offers reassurance and practical advice on identifying—and putting a stop to—any paranormal activity that's creeping you out. Discover how to rule out any earthly explanations for strange phenomena. A comprehensive overview of all kinds of hauntings and ghosts—from aggressive poltergeists to harmless family spirits to malevolent demons—will help you understand and identify your unearthly houseguest. If you still want to banish your ghost, you'll find plenty of simple, effective techniques to get the job done.

Is Your House Haunted? also offers advice on how to talk to children about ghosts and when it might be necessary to call in paranormal experts.

978-0-7387-2681-6, 240pp., 5¼ x 8   **$14.95**

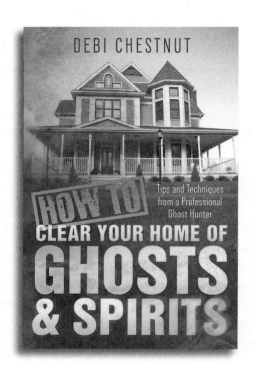

DEBI CHESTNUT

HOW TO

Tips and Techniques
from a Professional
Ghost Hunter

CLEAR YOUR HOME OF

GHOSTS
& SPIRITS

How to Clear Your Home of Ghosts & Spirits
Tips and Techniques from a Professional Ghost Hunter
DEBI CHESTNUT

When it comes to spooks, specters, and things that go bump in the night, knowledge is power and fear is the enemy. *How to Clear Your Home of Ghosts & Spirits* is a guide to everything you need to know about how to get rid of ghosts. Paranormal researcher Debi Chestnut provides a brief history of ghosts, and describes the types of ghosts, the different kinds of hauntings, the reasons ghosts haunt, and tips and techniques for clearing them.

Also discussed are important topics such as how ghosts and spirits can be brought into the home accidently, activities to avoid so as not to invite ghosts, and information on when and how to choose a paranormal team for extreme cases. Written in a no-nonsense style by an author with years of experience, this guide is a must-have for those who prefer to live with the facts instead of living in fear.

978-0-7387-3931-1, 240pp., 5¼ x 8   **$15.99**

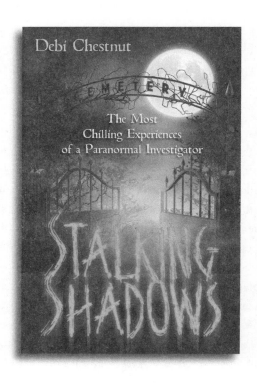

Debi Chestnut

CEMETERY

The Most
Chilling Experiences
of a Paranormal Investigator

STALKING
SHADOWS

Stalking Shadows
The Most Chilling Experiences of a Paranormal Investigator
DEBI CHESTNUT

If the world of the paranormal were a house, *Stalking Shadows* would be its wicked basement. And like a basement full of sinister energy, this collection of true stories is powerful enough to snuff out your flashlight, leaving you trembling in the darkness.

Join psychic medium and paranormal investigator Debi Chestnut as she explores twelve terrifying true encounters with ghosts, dark beings, and negative entities. Discover an abandoned house of horrors that becomes more evil with every victim it claims. Follow a tortured spirit trapped in a forsaken mirror. Feel the savage pain of a distraught ghost that screams out in agony. Once you descend into the paranormal basement, you'll uncover the true lives of the dead—in thrilling ways you never expected.

978-0-7387-3943-4, 216 pp., 5¼ x 8   **$15.99**

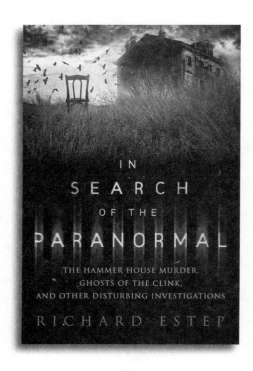

IN SEARCH OF THE PARANORMAL

THE HAMMER HOUSE MURDER, GHOSTS OF THE CLINK, AND OTHER DISTURBING INVESTIGATIONS

RICHARD ESTEP

In Search of the Paranormal
*The Hammer House Murder, Ghosts of the Clink,
and Other Disturbing Investigations*
RICHARD ESTEP

From exploring the Tower of London to investigating a haunted Colorado firehouse, paranormal researcher Richard Estep takes you behind the scenes for an up-close-and-personal encounter with a fascinating legion of hauntings. This collection reveals some of the most chilling, captivating, and weird cases that Richard has investigated over the past twenty years, in England and in the United States.

In Search of the Paranormal is filled with rich historical detail, present-day research, and compelling eyewitness accounts. You are there with the team at each haunted location: walking through a desecrated graveyard, shivering in a dark basement, getting thrown into The Clink, watching a "ghost-lit" stage in an old theater. Employing a variety of investigative methods—from high-tech gadgets to old-fashioned practices such as dowsing, table tipping, and Ouija boards—Richard Estep and his team uncover the dark mysteries of the paranormal realm.

978-0-7387-4488-9, 264 pp., 5¼ x 8   **$15.99**

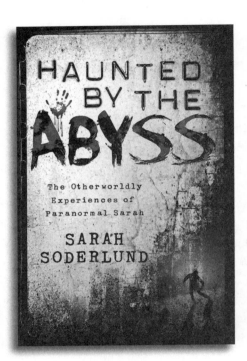

HAUNTED
BY THE
ABYSS

The Otherworldly
Experiences of
Paranormal Sarah

SARAH
SODERLUND

Haunted by the Abyss
The Otherworldly Experiences of Paranormal Sarah
SARAH SODERLUND

Journey into the terrifying abyss, where malevolent spirits and otherworldly beasts lurk. From childhood experiences with demons and aliens to a Missouri cemetery filled with phantom drums and territorial ghosts, these first-hand accounts of paranormal phenomena will chill your bones and thrill your mind.

Sarah Soderlund, also known as Paranormal Sarah, has been psychically gifted since childhood. Her intuitive abilities, coupled with her education and extensive astral world investigative skills, provide a unique and fascinating perspective into the supernatural. She describes not only what happened in her haunted childhood home, but also why some houses are "alive" and how ghost energy can slam doors, whisper your name, or even manifest as a full-blown or partial apparition. *Haunted by the Abyss* takes you deep into Sarah's investigations, where you'll discover that these stories aren't just scary ... they're real.

978-0-7387-4589-3 , 240 pp., 5¼ x 8   **$15.99**
